Dreams in the Desert

By Daniel Layden

Table of Contents

Acknowledgments

I have been blessed by so many in my life. This book is about a rough period of my life in my twenties. So, I want to thank my friends and family at that time. I also want to thank many of the priests in my life at that time: The Reverend Jackie Matisse, The Reverend Canon Jason Leo, The Very Reverend Jim Leo, The Reverend Don Peterson, and The Reverend Pete Streimer. I also want to thank the two most influential priests in my life as I grew up at Saint George's Episcopal Church in Dayton, Ohio: The Reverend James Paget and The Reverend Bill Bumiller.

I have been blessed to be a part of some amazing Christian communities. I want to thank all the people of Saint George's Dayton and the other churches I have served during the events described in this book: Saint John's Episcopal Church Columbus, Ohio and Christ Church Cathedral Cincinnati, Ohio. Further, I was blessed to be a part of an incredible camp program through the Episcopal Diocese of Southern Ohio at Procter Camp and Conference Center. I will always count Bob, Scott, Neal, Victoria, Lori, Christiane, Kathryn, Sally, and Karen as special brothers and sisters in Christ.

While writing this manuscript I received a great deal of feedback from some wonderful people at Saint Alban's Episcopal Church in Fort Wayne, Indiana. I especially want to thank Judith Palmer for going through the manuscript multiple times and offering many valuable suggestions. Also, a big thank you to Melissa Renner and my brother Jim for helping me during the final stages to print this book.

Huge thanks also to my seminary professors at Virginia Theological Seminary in Alexandria, Virginia. They taught me a great deal about scripture and ethics. Specifically I want to thank The Reverend Dr. Katherine Grieb, The Reverend Dr. John Yieh, Dr. Stephen Cook, and Dr. Timothy Sedgwick.

Finally, this book and my journey were most influenced by three incredible people: my Dad, my Mom, and Nancy Grimes. My parents were always extremely dedicated and loving to my brothers and me. Nancy was a gifted dream analyst taught in the Jungian institute in Switzerland. More important than being a great analyst, she was an even more amazing Christian mentor and fellow seeker. She was my guiding angel in my darkest time.

This book is written for all those who seek God and a deeper inner knowledge of God. I especially dedicate this book to my incredible daughters Anna and Lydia. May they and others one day more fully know the inner life which is a gift from God.

Introduction

"On a Dark Winding Road" Thursday 9/8/94

I dreamed I was leaving High School and I couldn't remember where I parked my car. I looked everywhere and then I wondered if I even drove. I ran into a girl who was driving. She knew exactly where my car was and how I got to school that morning. So we hopped into my car and started driving. We drove around some really treacherous roads in the dark. I often could not see where we were going.

My Prayer

My great prayer with this book is that by sharing my journey, others may see God more clearly in their own. Everybody has their own journey, and we experience different things at different times in life. This book chronicles my spiritual journey during my mid-twenties, a tremendously formative time for everyone. For me it was a particularly painful time. I believe my experiences may help others at different points on their spiritual journey. When we share our stories and how God touches our lives, then we help one another.

I hope you will see that the underlying force in this book is the Holy Spirit. It is the Holy Spirit who guides and prompts us to become aware and respond to the inner life.

This book is about Christian spirituality and dreams. I would not expect that everybody who reads this will enter into such great depth of dream analysis. However, I do hope this book brings awareness to the power of exploring your dreams. In chapter four I offer some simple questions each person can use to do this. Dreams are like great paintings. The more you look at, play with, and not force meaning into them, the more grace you will receive.

My deep inner pain

The deep inner anxiety and pain that prompted and dominated my journey during the time of this book can never be adequately described; I try to describe it as best I can without making it the sole focus. The thoughts and images I had dominated my mind all the time. That was me and my experience. Yours will be uniquely your own. There is no way to compare them, nor should we try. We experience what we experience. Further, one does not have to experience anxiety and pain to embark on an inward spiritual journey, although people who experience a kind of 'desert' or 'dark night of the soul' are often guided to greater spiritual awareness. This is just what happened to me. Whatever your current state and mindset, you can always benefit by paying attention to your inner Spiritual journey and your dreams.

Timeframe of this book

The events in this book start in the Autumn of 1993 and end in the Autumn of 1995. I was 22 years old and starting my senior year in college as the book begins. I connect with Nancy in late Summer of 1994. The dreams and analysis in this book take place in the first year after meeting Nancy. I did, however, continue in dream analysis for several years. The initial dark anxiety and raw questioning described in this book ended in 1995, but I continued to enjoy doing inner dream analysis with Nancy. There were many other, albeit smaller, ups and downs over those years.

The People in this book

In this book I talk about several people in my life at the time I went through this journey. I have changed their names where possible. Further, this book does not give a full picture of anyone I highlight. My thoughts about each person are just that, my thoughts. They are only from my own perspective and often are not my full thoughts on that person. All the people in this book are wonderful people. I have been truly blessed in my life with the people I have known. In some parts of this book I highlight certain characteristics of people I know that may cast them in a negative light. However, this is not done to disparage that person, but it is because I was learning about something in myself that they represented.

However, it is impossible to protect the identity of some of my family, especially my mom and dad. It is important to note that my mom and dad are both extremely wonderful, caring and devoted parents. However, like all parents they are not perfect. To be true to my journey, I have to point out some of their shortcomings as I experienced them. As I write this book years after the events, I am now a parent myself. I know I have many shortcomings that will impact my two daughters. I pray I am half as dedicated to them as my parents were to me.

I am a guy

I state the obvious. I am a guy. This book is about my spiritual journey, as a man. However, this is not just a book for men. Many of the teachings can benefit anyone. The lessons that are particular to me as a man have similar parallels in the growth of women. I do hope that a woman can learn and benefit from many of the things I highlight in my journey.

The Bible passages in this book

Every chapter in this book begins with scripture. I am, after all, a Christian and an Episcopal priest. It is second nature for me to start most everything with scripture. I do strongly believe that the scripture passages highlighted in this book help to explain the inner processes of each chapter. The Bible passages do not always explicitly relate to the subject (for example nowhere in the Bible does it directly talk about a 'mother complex' or 'anima'). However, I do believe that you can look at many passages in the Bible with an eye on the inner psychological life. Most importantly I always pray I do scripture justice when I preach or write. I hope that is the case here. All scriptures quoted in this book are from the 2011 New International Version.

My reflections

My reflections about the Bible passages are my reflections from years of Biblical study and exegesis. I am not a New or Old

Testament scholar. I am a priest who tries to find meaning and relate it so that it may benefit others. My thoughts on the passages in this book were surely inspired by many commentators and others.

I try to look at the passages from an inner perspective. I could not have written these reflections in 1996 or 1997. Granted, I learned the initial inner depth psychological lessons in 1994 and 1995. However, the lessons I began to learn had to marinate in my mind for many years. My seminary experience helped me tremendously in my thoughts as well. It is important to note that this book is written twenty-three years after the initial lessons, so I pray there is greater wisdom to the reflections on the scriptures as a result.

The Dreams Analyzed

At the end of most chapters I share a personal dream I had. They are all from 1994 when I first began dream analysis. Many of these dreams have stuck in my mind for years. They are presented in this book exactly as I wrote them in my journal all those years ago (except for a very few corrections). I wanted to present the material from my unconscious as raw and truthfully as I could. The other journal notes are also straight out of my journals from years ago.

After each dream there is a conversation between Nancy and me. These are not word for word how our sessions really went. I tried to represent what we did talk about as best I could recall though. I looked at my notes from each dream and tried to be true to how I remember Nancy and me at that time.

I spent almost twenty years with Nancy in analysis. I can close my eyes, and still see her face and hear her voice. She was always very caring and even humorous at times. She was also not afraid to challenge me. Overall she was extremely wise, and she never tried to dictate things. She was a spiritual lady who let God and the unconscious dream material lead. I hope that comes through in the way I wrote up the conversations.

As I say, I participated in dream analysis for almost twenty years. I have two trunks of notebooks. Over a long time you can really see how things progress in your dreams. It is important to note that I am not a trained analyst, but I am an expert on my Spiritual journey as you are on yours. I pray this book may be a blessing to others, as I have been truly blessed. May the God who is awake, alive, active, and moving be made aware in you.

Reflection questions

At the end of each chapter there are a few reflection questions. They are designed to help you reflect on your Spiritual life in relation to the topic of each chapter. They can be something you can reflect on your own or with a group.

May 8th 2019

Chapter One: Entering the Desert

Then Jesus was led by the Spirit into the wilderness to be tempted by the devil. After fasting forty days and forty nights, he was hungry. The tempter came to him and said, "If you are the Son of God, tell these stones to become bread." Jesus answered, "It is written: 'Man shall not live on bread alone, but on every word that comes from the mouth of God.'" Then the devil took him to the holy city and had him stand on the highest point of the temple. "If you are the Son of God," he said, "throw yourself down. For it is written: "'He will command his angels concerning you, and they will lift you up in their hands, so that you will not strike your foot against a stone.'" Jesus answered him, "It is also written: 'Do not put the Lord your God to the test.'" Again, the devil took him to a very high mountain and showed him all the kingdoms of the world and their splendor. "All this I will give you," he said, "if you will bow down and worship me." Jesus said to him, "Away from me, Satan! For it is written: 'Worship the Lord your God, and serve him only.'" Then the devil left him, and angels came and attended him. (Matthew 4:1-11, NIV)

I can still remember when and where it happened. It was Thursday September 30th of 1993 on an Avenue just northeast of my college campus. I was beginning my senior year and I was walking home from a religious studies class I had just recently started. The religious studies department was agnostic at best. Well, after all, it was a public university. However, I had grown up with the Christian faith. I wanted to get a religious studies minor to go with my Psychology major because I loved God. I loved exploring all things about God, religious thought, and experience. I was a strong Christian believer. Moreover, I was one who practiced my faith. I believed God truly was with me.

I often consulted what I describe as an inner presence or guiding light that I called my, 'God-voice.' It was not a separate voice that I heard, but a calming, thoughtful presence or light within that seemed to help guide me, especially in times of need. I trusted it. I firmly believed that God was with me. I believed that God would direct me if I listened to this inner guidance, this loving companion, this 'God-voice' that I had sensed most of my life. Oh, sure, I did not always consult or pay attention to it. I was far from being an angel. However, like an old friend my 'God-voice' was there to comfort me when I needed guidance.

Now, on the streets of Columbus, I would literally feel my 'God-voice' ripped away. It was like walking deep into a desert. My insides started to feel drier, anxious, and barren. My brain was filled with all these academic questions about God. "Do I truly know who God is?" I started to wonder. I started to doubt. As the questions mounted in my head, my anxiety increased. My head was suddenly and rudely filled with a cacophony of questions and doubts. "God are you with me?" "Are you real?" "I can't feel you!" "Did I do something wrong?" "Oh, my God, am I still a Christian?" Nothing but naked, bare, dry, anxious silence greeted my inner voice now. "Are you in there?" "Oh, Lord, give me guidance!!"

Jesus is with us in the Desert

There are multiple desert or wilderness experiences in the Bible. Forty days and forty nights is a long time. All of these experiences eventually led those who experienced them to deeper relationship with God. Noah had to wonder if his watery desert would ever end. Moses led the people out of Egypt straight into a desert experience that would last for forty *years*. Even Jesus was significantly shaped by a desert experience.

After fasting for forty days and forty nights, Jesus is visited by the devil. The devil first tempts him because of his current hungry condition. The devil says, "If you are the Son of God, tell these stones to become bread." (Matthew 4:3) Jesus replies, "It is written: 'Man shall not live on bread alone, but on every word that comes from the mouth of God.'" (Matthew 4:4) The devil then tempts Jesus using scripture. ""If you are the Son of God,' he said, 'throw yourself down. For it is written: "*He will command his angels concerning you, and they will lift you up in their hands, so that you will not strike your foot against a stone.*"" (Matthew 4:6) Jesus said to him, "It is also written: 'Do not put the Lord your God to the test.'" (Matthew 4:7) The devil finally tempts him with the lure of power. "Again, the devil took him to a very high

2

mountain and showed him all the kingdoms of the world and their splendor. 'All this I will give you,' he said, 'if you will bow down and worship me.'" (Matthew 4:8, 9) Jesus sternly replies, "Away from me, Satan! For it is written: 'Worship the Lord your God, and serve him only.'" (Matthew 4:10)

Jesus stays consistent. He knows not only the words of scripture, but the love and intent of scripture. Jesus is tempted in the only unique way Jesus could have been tempted. Now, none of us is Jesus, but I believe we are each tempted in our own individual ways. Sometimes we go through desert experiences that can help shape and deepen our faith life. It does not say in the text if Jesus completely felt alone or abandoned by God. I for one believe that Jesus did experience a sense of separation. I believe he experienced this agony here in the desert, in the Garden, and during periods on the cross. When we experience the desert, we may feel abandoned as well. However, the great blessing of Jesus' temptation is that even if we cannot feel God's love and comfort, God is there with us because Christ has been there. Moreover, like Jesus, we are often led by the Holy Spirit into such times solely for the purpose of deepening our faith life and Spiritual awareness. Now when we are in those places we cannot realize this. We cannot see "the forest for the trees" as the old saying goes. We only feel the dryness, abandonment, and anxiety. However, God's love is all around us. You could not have told me this truth when I began my intense desert experience, but in hindsight I found it to be true.

The seeds of faith originally planted in me

As long as I can remember I have thought about God. I was brought to church from my birth by my mom. I loved going to church. Saint George's was a wonderful place to grow up in the faith. It was always my second home.

As a little boy I loved to go to chapel. The chapel was filled with love. There was a great portrait of Jesus as the Good Shepherd hanging on the wall. This is where I first felt the love and presence of God. Outside the window, during Sunday School, I would look out on the grass and picture Jesus with me. I could actually sense his presence. I can remember there was a statue of Saint Francis of Assisi on the hill. Over in the corner was a bush. There was an opening between the wall and the bush. I actually thought of that opening as the opening to the empty tomb.

It was during this innocent and formative time that I first sensed the 'God-voice' within. "God is real." "Jesus is alive." "He is Risen indeed." My priest was Reverend Rick. None of us could pronounce his last name well, so we called him Mr. B. Mr. B would pray out loud. He would actually talk to God out loud. He had this big booming voice. I could remember him shouting out to God every morning at Vacation Bible School and during chapel. "Good morning, God!" We would all repeat, "Good morning, God." He would then pray to God about a few things. Then he would end with, "Well God, I got a lot to do today, but we'll talk to you later. I may forget about you, but I know you will never forget about me."

I thought to myself, "This is a God I can talk to, like a real live friend." I thus learned to talk to God in my thoughts. I would do it a lot. I would ask God in my thoughts what I should do. The voice I often sensed was not another external voice, but a thoughtful presence I trusted. It seemed to come from a different place inside me. I learned to always trust my 'God-voice.'

Back to 1993

Now it was gone. Questioning one's faith is not a bad thing. In fact it is a very good thing. I learned in our church to question our faith so it could become stronger. What I began to experience now was different, however. This was way more intense than reflecting on questions about God's character. This was more about the deep basic questions about God's existence. Did I really trust the presence of a living God that dwells in the world and within?

As I walked along, stuck with philosophical questions about God in my head, I felt like my faith was ripped away from me. I kept thinking and thinking, over and over. I was trapped in my thoughts. "Where did you go, God?" "Where is that 'God-voice' I learned to trust?" "Did I lose faith?" "Was it my fault?" Anxiety and fear gripped me.

This was the beginning of an over two-year ordeal of intense desert dryness. During this time I would learn much. It was a journey through the desert, learning how God is faithful to us even if we do not know it.

My journal became my life

I began to journal early in this process. It helped me stay focused. Later, it helped me see where I had been. Often we see God in the rear view mirror more than in the present. The following is something I wrote while I was in this dark space:

"God either exists or God does not exist, whether I believe in God or not. Jesus Christ was either crucified and resurrected or He was not, whether I believe it or not. Jesus says that no one shall come to the Father but by me. Problem…other religions. Jesus says repent for the end is near. What does near mean? God either created the world or God did not? I watched a tape on Near death Experiences. In those experiences there were many similarities. However, Christians saw Christian symbols while Hindu's saw Hindu symbols. Well this means that that is the way it speaks to you. But, if no one shall come to the Father, but by me, this presents a problem for someone who does not know Jesus. What happens to someone who does not know Jesus? Thus, is it all just a manifestation in our minds? Does it exist simply because we believe it does, not because it really does? Analysis. Every Human being has basic needs: food, water, air, etc. Is the soul just another need that is taken care of on earth? When we die does it die? What makes it so special? When I am hungry I think of food that I know exists. When we die, does our need for food for the soul die? Results of these questions: 1. God is either working in me to change me (I hope so) 2. I am going to go crazy with it. 3. It just doesn't matter.

I was trapped by questions. Questions I could simply not let go. I was haunted by the questions night and day. They never left me. I could never feel comfortable with an answer or inside myself. When I had questioned things about faith in the past, I could always let it go or feel satisfied with an answer I discovered. My 'God-voice' would help me. Now it was gone. There seemed to be no answers to these questions. I felt like darkness was over me all the time. I could never be free or at peace.

I struggled with the following questions: 1. Did God create? 2. Was Jesus Christ raised from the dead? 3. What happens to those who did not believe in Jesus Christ? There did not seem to be definite answers. I was obsessed with finding the correct, complete answer. I remember thinking if I could just prove that Jesus Christ was raised from the dead, or if I could just prove that creation happened, and then I could be at peace again. I devoured books like *More than a Carpenter* by Josh McDowell; *Science and The Bible* by Henry Morris; *Mere Christianity* by C.S. Lewis; *Did Jesus Rise from the Dead: The Resurrection Debate* by Gary Habermas and Antony Flew. All this was great reading, but I could not quiet the storm inside of me. They did not give me the definite answers I craved.

Seeking the wisdom of others

At first I was afraid to tell my Christian friends about my doubts. I felt like there was something wrong with me. I felt like I must have lost faith. How could I tell them? I avoided talking about it with my friends. I felt jealous when I was around other Christians. "If only I could have their faith," I would think. They seemed so happy. I was almost angry when I saw their joy. It angered me deep within.

Finally, I knew I had to trust someone, so I trusted an old friend and mentor from my high school youth group. He tried to ease my thoughts to let me know everyone had doubts. He told me about an author named Frederick Buechner who talked about doubt not being in opposition to faith, but a part of it. "Doubts are the Ants in the pants of faith. They keep it awake and moving." [1]

What was truly extraordinary about Buechner's writing is that one of my former priests, Reverend John, quoted him often. Reverend John had actually told my high school youth worker about Buechner's writings. Reverend John had died a few years earlier while I was a sophomore in college. Now it was like my old priest and father figure was speaking to me through Frederick Buechner.

The darkness, however, was not lifted. I could simply not let go of the questions. Buechner's writings were beautiful and helped, but they were not the cure. I wanted my living faith back. I wanted that voice, presence, and light from God within me to return.

The next thing I tried was to seek counsel. I asked my current priest. He recommended another priest for counseling. I

[1] Buechner, *Wishful Thinking: A Theological ABC*, 20.

remember thinking this was it. This is what will cure me. I can still remember when Reverend Ben opened the door. He had had a stroke and retired early from active parish ministry. His mind however was as sharp as ever. "It's your nickel," he said. I went about spilling my guts. He told me that it was usual for someone to lose their innocent childhood faith. This was a natural process. He also told me that a dark night of the soul, or desert experience, could actually be a good thing. Finally, he said that when he had dark times he always found his faith again in the community. In the community? I had been avoiding Christian community because I felt like something was wrong. His words, however, caused me to rethink that. I needed to get out there and find my own community. The questions did not cease, the anxiety did not cease, but I felt like I had a plan now.

Reflection questions:
1. How did your faith life begin?
2. When have you struggled with your faith? Have you ever had a desert experience?
3. How does Jesus' life inform and affect yours?

Chapter Two: Go West Young Man

Now there was a Pharisee, a man named Nicodemus who was a member of the Jewish ruling council. He came to Jesus at night and said, "Rabbi, we know that you are a teacher who has come from God. For no one could perform the signs you are doing if God were not with him." Jesus replied, "Very truly I tell you, no one can see the kingdom of God unless they are born again." "How can someone be born when they are old?" Nicodemus asked. "Surely they cannot enter a second time into their mother's womb to be born!" Jesus answered, "Very truly I tell you, no one can enter the kingdom of God unless they are born of water and the Spirit. Flesh gives birth to flesh, but the Spirit gives birth to spirit. You should not be surprised at my saying, 'You must be born again.' The wind blows wherever it pleases. You hear its sound, but you cannot tell where it comes from or where it is going. So it is with everyone born of the Spirit." "How can this be?" Nicodemus asked. "You are Israel's teacher," said Jesus, "and do you not understand these things?" (John 3:1-10, NIV)

This is quite possibly my favorite passage in all of scripture. I love the phrase about the wind blows wherever it pleases. You hear its sound, but you cannot tell where it comes from or where it is going. This, Jesus tells us, is what life is like for one who is "born of the Spirit." No one can say where a gust of wind begins or exactly where it is headed. You can only be caught up by it. You can only feel the rush, the coolness, and the refreshment of the wind. You can hear the sound of the wind. You can see the things the wind moves. However, you cannot see or capture the wind.

Nicodemus was not one who understood this yet. He was caught in the rational. He was trapped in his head trying to understand deep Spiritual matters with external physical realities and logic. He wanted 2 plus 2 to equal 4, and 2 plus 2 does equal 4. However, in the world of the Spirit it is not experienced in the same way. Things add up in the Spiritual world, but it is more about relationship, process, and love. Nicodemus does not know this yet, but he will.

Little does Nicodemus know, but his encounter with Jesus is a birth. By the end of John's gospel, we see Nicodemus as one who helps Joseph of Arimathea wrap Jesus' body after his death on the cross. Something begins to move in Nicodemus the night he first encounters Jesus. He begins to be touched by the Spirit. He begins to notice the wind in his life, in his heart.

Trying to understand the Spirit externally and rationally

In the winter of 1994 I was much like Nicodemus. I wanted to have everything logically explained. I had struggled with questions about creation, resurrection, and other faith traditions. I wanted the answers. I was stuck saying much like Nicodemus, "Surely they cannot enter a second time into their mother's womb to be born!'" (John 3:4) I kept asking, "Did God create? Was Jesus resurrected? What happens to people of other faiths?" Little did I know at the time, the wind of the Holy Spirit was beginning to blow in my life. I did not sense this wind all around me, but I was beginning to be transformed. It seemed like a violent wind at first, but it was still the loving wind of the Spirit. It was starting to move things, disrupt things.

I felt the wind. I heard it rush around me. I could see the dead leaves in my life begin to shimmer, but I thought it was all only darkness and painful anxiety. I certainly did not know where this wind of the Spirit came from or where it was going. I could not let go of the questions, and in a way, it was God not letting me let go of the journey that God prepared for me.

My life crumbles

As the winter went on that year, my life seemed to go from bad to worse. My relationship with my girlfriend deteriorated. I was often too quiet and too withdrawn. It was hard to be in relationship with me. Furthermore, I was jealous. I was jealous of what all my friends seemed to have, namely… a strong faith. I wanted to feel like a believing Christian again so I could enjoy time with my friends.

A few days before Valentine's day, my girlfriend called it quits. I couldn't blame her really. I still cared for her, but I was stuck. I had to get right on the inside. I figured I would take

Reverend Ben's advice and try to find my faith again in Christian community.

I found a group of friends who wanted to start a Bible study. "This is it," I thought. Now we are getting somewhere. It was a wonderful group of friends. A few of these friends had been camp counselors with me a few summers before. A few others I knew from other friends. It was great. We met once a week to discuss the Bible. We had a work booklet to guide us through the scriptures. I forget what the work booklet was titled, and I have since misplaced it. However, it was the conversations that I treasured. Each person in the group had a great faith. I think they knew I was struggling, and for the first time it felt OK to struggle with them. These are the type of friends you really want.

However, I still could not turn off the nagging doubts in my mind. Every time someone would offer a good thought, inside my head I would contradict it, or think of something negative. I would go home from our sessions happy to be with my friends, but frustrated that I could not stop the nagging doubts and negative thoughts in my head. I even became aware of answers to some of my nagging questions, but it never seemed like 2 plus 2 equaled 4. Does it really add up?

Rational answers to nagging questions

I did resolve some of my big philosophical religious issues in my mind. I realized on the question of creation, that God indeed could have created. Science was not proof that creation did not happen. The theory of evolution without God was not the final answer. I came to realize that a creative force could definitely have been guiding all the science and evolution. It actually makes a great deal of sense that a creative intelligent force is what has been guiding the development of the cosmos. Further, even if one can show scientifically how life began, that would not mean that God was not creatively guiding that process. Just because one cannot see a God figure looking like an old man with a white beard molding things out of mud, doesn't mean that God did not and does not create. One can see the effects of God through the life force, without seeing God physically as a being.

Further, the stories of creation in the Bible speak about truth, not just historical fact. The truth of the six days creation is that God continually brings greater and greater order to the universe. It is not to be taken literally. The truth is that God

11

continues to separate and give greater order. God separates the light from the darkness, separates the waters, and separates the land from the waters. Genesis is not meant to be a scientific treatise. It is best understood as almost poetic truth telling about a God who creates by bringing greater order and purpose.

In a similar way, the Adam and Eve story tells the truth about humanity's condition. That is we are separated from God because of lack of trust and pride. It is the story of broken relationship and thus separation. Whether Adam and Eve actually historically lived or not is not the point. It is the truth of the story that matters. We were created and our relationship with God is broken.

I could also explain about the resurrection. I could never prove the resurrection actually happened unless I was there, but I could trust the witness of the apostles. Many authors write about whether Jesus was telling the truth, lying, or was simply crazy. Actually it is the veracity of those who wrote about Jesus that is in question. Did they make it up? Did they exaggerate? If so, why? Or was it a legend that developed over time? I can always go back to a few certainties. One, It would have been very hard for all those people to live out the lie that Jesus was resurrected if he was not. They all believed in God and as good Jews they would have known that to claim Jesus as Lord, if he was not, would be blasphemous. Would all those people have put their eternal souls in jeopardy to perpetuate a lie about a false messiah? Two, they were too profound in their writings about Jesus' teachings to be complete liars, hoaxsters, or lunatics. How could someone write about such profound things as the good Samaritan, the lost sheep, the prodigal son, and then completely lie about the central teaching, namely that Jesus rose from the dead. Third, why would they die for a made-up faith? Hoaxsters generally are not martyrs? Finally, how could they have been so honest in how they are portrayed in the gospel stories and in the book of Acts if they were not genuine people? Usually people who are making something up would also make themselves look very, very good. In the gospels, the followers of Jesus are anything but perfect heroes. In fact, they are often bumbling idiots constantly making mistakes. All this adds up to one thing...we can trust the witness of the earliest Christians who actually experienced the resurrection.

Furthermore, the writers of the New Testament were too close to the events to have either made it up or to have misinterpreted the events they experienced or were told about. The time from

12

the events themselves to when they were written down was not long enough for legend to have developed. The central message of, "He Is Risen," is what shaped the ever spreading Christian community from the beginning. A comparable time frame for us to think about are the events of Martin Luther King, Jr.'s life. It is about the same time frame between the event of the resurrection and the writings of the gospels to the events of Martin Luther King, Jr.'s life and our time now. Would those who followed Martin Luther King, Jr. have completely developed whole new fantastical stories, or can we trust their witness to events, big events, twenty, thirty, or forty years after the fact? Of course we can trust them. Legends do not grow up that quickly about the major central events. The central event of the resurrection would be well remembered. "He is Risen!" is the message that shaped the community from the beginning, and then later the writings were produced. Sure, there would be difference of details around the main events, and some further elaboration of what was happening. This is, in fact, what we see in the Gospels and other New Testament writings, but the central facts remain consistent. "He is Risen!" was always the core message.

In addition to all this, there is the whole matter of the Holy Spirit growing the church. The early church grew in amazing ways, and the early Christians were honest about how some rejected the message while some accepted it. They also wrote about some of the problems and controversies in the earliest Christian communities. All this is to point out that the early church was not lead by hoaxsters, lunatics, or misinformed daydreamers. Result, I trust their witness about the resurrection of Jesus Christ.

Finally, I had a rational explanation about other faiths. The writings of Frederick Buechner were key to my thoughts here. Buechner unpacked, in a new way for me, the phrase, "I am the way and the truth and the life. No one comes to the Father except through me." (John 14:6) Buechner pointed out that one could be on Jesus' way, with his truth and life in them even if they had never known the name of Jesus Christ.[2] This was a revelation to me. Now I could say people like Ghandi were a part of God's salvation because they indeed had the mark of Christ on their lives. Further, someone who lived long ago, and thus never heard about Jesus, could also have the mark of Christ on their life. This seemed to me to be a much more inclusive way of looking at

---

[2] Buechner, *Wishful Thinking: A Theological ABC*, 14.

this issue. In the end salvation is left up to the Lord, but Buechner cracked the door open in my mind for the salvation of others who perhaps did not directly profess the Christian faith.

Still spiritually in the darkness

However, even with all these answers to the three questions I was struggling with, I still felt in darkness. I still did not feel God in my soul. I could not fully sense the warmth and comfort of a caring wind. It was there, but I did not understand that the wind isn't always warm and comfortable. Sometimes it seems cold and violent to shake up our lives.

In many ways I came up with the rational answers to the questions I was struggling with, but I had not fully been born of water and the Spirit. God was working in me, but I could not see it. I was being touched by Christian community, but I could not see that either. I was stuck in the external, unable to connect to the internal. I was stuck in my head, unable to connect to my heart.

My senior year nears an end

As Winter turned into Spring I was nearing graduation. I was excited to graduate, but what would I do? I remember sitting in the enclosed balcony at the house I shared with four other guys. I listened to a concert in the distance, and I wondered what to do next in life. I became very anxious. What kind of job could I do? I would receive a Bachelor of Science in Psychology. A good degree, but I would most likely need to get more specific education or training. I did not know what I wanted to do. I remember at commencement being in the largest college (Arts and Sciences) in the largest major (Psychology) at one of the largest Universities. I remember thinking to myself, "Boy, I feel really unique and special...not."

The wind blows West

Before I graduated I received a mailing from my church. It was a brochure about a Christian ministry in the National Parks. "Now this looks interesting," I thought. The ministry would entail going and working in a national park, and offering worship services to travelers. During the week I'd work at a gas station. On the weekends I'd pair up with a ministry partner. We would go around the campgrounds and invite people to an ecumenical Christian service of music and teaching. It was not something long term, but it was something I might love to do. I loved being outside. I also loved being around others who were talking about and worshipping God. I applied and was placed to go to Yellowstone National Park. "Go West young man," was all I kept thinking.

I was excited, but I did have worries. Worry number one was how could I preach about Jesus, when inside I still felt like I struggled with my faith. Worry number two was how could I find community?

After graduation I drove my father's car out to Yellowstone. I packed my bags in the car and hit I-70 to go west. I kept thinking that maybe I could find myself out West. Maybe the nagging doubts would go away.

However, when I arrived instead of things getting better, they simply got worse. I worked at a gas station in the most remote place in the park. People would come by and ask, "Where can I go see the bears?" They all wanted to meet Yogi. I would tell them to hope and pray that they would only see the bears and the bison at a great distance. Maulings were not uncommon and the bison could gore you and throw you around like a ragdoll. Sadly, some people are too dumb for their own good. This was the only lesson I felt like I was learning.

On Saturdays, my ministry partner and I would go around to camp sites and invite people to a camp side church service. I loved being outside, but I could not get anything out of the service. I wondered, "Did these people see right through me and know that I had huge nagging doubts?" I felt a little hypocritical, but I wanted to believe. I wanted to believe more than anyone else, but why did God feel so far away? Why did I still feel barren, naked, and anxious all the time? I had felt this way constantly for nine months now. I was surrounded by all this natural beauty and I could not enjoy a minute of it.

The retreat back East

On the fourth of July, I decided to drive back home. It was a long drive for just one. I have never felt more alone than seeing others celebrating, being happy, and shooting off fireworks, as I drove along. I-70 can be a very lonely place, especially in

Kansas. I went west young man, and now I was retreating in defeat back east. "Something has got to work, PLEASE GOD," I thought in anguish.

Reflection questions:
1. What questions about God do you struggle with? How have you answered them at different times in your life?
2. When are you like Nicodemus being too literal and rational for your own good?
3. How has your experience of community shaped your faith life?

Chapter Three: Nourished by Living Water

So he came to a town in Samaria called Sychar, near the plot of ground Jacob had given to his son Joseph. Jacob's well was there, and Jesus, tired as he was from the journey, sat down by the well. It was about noon. When a Samaritan woman came to draw water, Jesus said to her, "Will you give me a drink?" (His disciples had gone into the town to buy food.) The Samaritan woman said to him, "You are a Jew and I am a Samaritan woman. How can you ask me for a drink?" (For Jews do not associate with Samaritans.) Jesus answered her, "If you knew the gift of God and who it is that asks you for a drink, you would have asked him and he would have given you living water." "Sir," the woman said, "you have nothing to draw with and the well is deep. Where can you get this living water? Are you greater than our father Jacob, who gave us the well and drank from it himself, as did also his sons and his livestock?" Jesus answered, "Everyone who drinks this water will be thirsty again, but whoever drinks the water I give them will never thirst. Indeed, the water I give them will become in them a spring of water welling up to eternal life." The woman said to him, "Sir, give me this water so that I won't get thirsty and have to keep coming here to draw water." (John 4:5-15, NIV)

What is that living water that Jesus says he will give that gushes up to eternal life? How do we access this well? The Samaritan woman says, "Sir, give me this water so that I won't get thirsty…" (John 4:15) I think we all want to be given this water. We all want to find the fountain of youth. We all desire eternal life, but can we really access this water?

It has often been pointed out that this is an unlikely encounter between the Samaritan woman and Jesus at the well. Jews rarely if ever conversed with Samaritans. Jews and Samaritans tended to despise each other for many reasons, too many to go into

17

here. Further, men rarely spoke to strange women, but Jesus does not hesitate to encounter this woman. Jesus is physically thirsty and he perceives that the woman is spiritually thirsty. Jesus the great rabbi seizes this teachable moment.

The woman on the other hand probably feels sorry for this man. She, too, knows it is not an encounter that is proper, but she sees he has no way to access the water deep in the well. Little does she know that she is actually the one who needs a bucket to go deep, deep into her soul. We too are often like the woman at the well. We know we are both physically and spiritually thirsty, but we keep focusing on the external physical thirst. We disregard the deeper inner thirst where Jesus can show us a well that will gush up to eternal life. God desperately wants us to lower the bucket into this well.

My thirst for the deep inner well

In the summer of 1994, I was thirsty and my soul was dry. I was trying to quench my soul by external means. I sought answers in books. I looked for guidance in community. I even went out West searching for truth. These are all good things and I am glad I did them. However, I needed to learn how to go deep within to draw up living water.

As I sat at the gas station in Yellowstone National Park, I was thirsty. I kept trying to think of how I might get out of this painful pattern of great negativity, anxiety, and doubt. I wanted to stop thinking and out-thinking myself. I wanted to stop feeling like I was on a small deserted island. "Lord, help me out of this dark dryness," I begged.

Back to Camp

After a few Sundays in Yellowstone, I could not take it anymore. I could not stand trying to preach about Jesus, while feeling barren inside. I decided to abandon the westward journey and go home. All told, I spent a month out west. I drove back by myself on the fourth of July. "Lord help me to find some comfort," was all I could think about. I decided to go back to where I had most recently experienced God on a deep level. I talked to my good friend and mentor who was in charge of the Diocesan summer camps, Reverend Debbie. She was the most spiritual person I knew. "Maybe Debbie can help set me straight," I

18

thought. I told her I could help out for room and board. She graciously and gladly welcomed me for the remainder of camp.

While I was back at camp, I met a new young vibrant priest. His name was Reverend Steve. Steve was to take over the camping program the next year from Debbie. More importantly for me Steve had a dad who was also a priest. His dad was looking to hire a youth minister. Steve set me up with an interview.

Becoming Quasimodo

I was hired and at the beginning of August 1994 I started work as the youth minister at a Cathedral in Cincinnati. "This will finally get me right," I thought. "I will be living in a Cathedral. I have to get right with God." I remembered what Buechner had written, "Generally speaking, if you want to know who you really are as distinct from who you like to think you are, keep an eye on where your feet take you."[3] This is a great quote and it is true, but I was still trying to solve an inner problem by changing the external.

My first few weeks at the Cathedral were miserable internally. I felt more anxious and darker than ever. The cathedral church was in downtown Cincinnati. My apartment was right under the bell tower. At any other time in my life I would have loved being there. I loved Cincinnati. I grew up in Dayton, Ohio. I was a huge Reds and Bengals fan, and downtown Cincinnati had so much to offer a young single guy.

However, I was not myself and I knew it. I remember sitting in my new apartment, staring at a cross on the wall for hours. I went from having anxious doubts about my faith in God, to suddenly having horrific images stuck in my head. All the images in my head were of pain, violence, and suffering. I could not get away from it. I would think of a horrible image and it would get stuck in my brain. "Get out, get out," I would cry to God to take away the awful images. "Oh, Lord, is this the pain of the cross?" I wondered in agony.

---

[3] Buechner, *Wishful Thinking: A Theological ABC*, 27.

I can't take it anymore

    I finally broke down and told someone I needed real help. The person I turned to was the woman who gave me life, my mom. My mom suggested that I go and see an analyst. Her name was Nancy. "Maybe Nancy could help," I thought.

    The first time I met with Nancy I knew I was going to be put on the right path. Not that God was not guiding my journey all along, but I definitely needed help finding some real living water. Everyone needs someone like Virgil from *The Divine Comedy* to guide them through the tough times.

    I told Nancy, after babbling about my problems for an hour, "I deeply want to feel the love of God in my life again. I want a living faith I can feel." I will never forget what she said next. She said, "I do not just believe in God, I know there is a God." I was stunned. What kind of confident faith was this? I could tell it was genuine as well. She told me to buy a notebook and write to God exactly what I deeply wanted and of what I was afraid. She also told me to write down my dreams, as much as I could remember. I rushed home, and that night I wrote out my wants and fears. Below is much of what I wrote.

What do I want?

- *I want to feel love.*
- *I want to feel you (God) there.*
- *I want to be a leader in your church.*
- *I want that skeptical voice gone.*
- *I want to be able to pray and get in touch with myself.*
- *I want to be around my friends and feel secure about my faith.*
- *I want to be able to talk about you (God) and not feel hypocritical.*
- *I want to be able to enjoy nature and not look at it and ask where did it come from.*
- *I want you to reveal yourself to me so that I know I am not projecting, but that it is really you (God).*
- *I want to be wounded.*
- *I want to be able to start over again and stumble upon God. I don't like to think I have been taught to believe something.*
- *I want to be able to stop and learn, not look and wonder.*
- *I want to be able to read the Bible and see you (God) in it, and not be frustrated by it.*

What am I afraid of:

- *I am afraid to grow old, lonely and bitter.*
- *I am afraid that I will never have any answers.*
- *I am afraid of losing all my friends.*
- *I am afraid of searching and finding nothing.*
- *I am afraid I can't help anyone anymore.*
- *I am afraid of hurting somebody.*

As I look back on these wants and fears now, I can still feel the raw emotion behind them. I think many people have had the same wants and fears. Knowing the great negative voice and images stuck in my head back then, I can see that it was good to clarify what I wanted and of what I was afraid. It was, in a great sense, lowering the bucket into a deep well, hoping to start the flow of water.

Paying attention to the unconscious

The first night I recorded my dreams was Tuesday August 23rd 1994. I remembered three dreams. I was always good at remembering my dreams. There are two tricks I use to remember my dreams. First, I pray to God, "Lord, teach me through my dreams." There is something to desiring to want to remember your dreams. You have to want to pay attention. The second trick is to write down your dreams right away. Have a notebook on your nightstand with a pen. If you wake up in the middle of the night, scribble a few important words that will help you recall the dreams. Once you wake up in the morning, jot down keywords to help you remember your dreams. Then write them out as best you can. If you do not remember everything, then write down what you do remember. The more you do this, the more you will remember. It is like anything else. Most people can get good at this. The problem is that many people wake up and immediately start thinking of all they have to do that day.

The first night I journaled my dreams I remembered three dreams. One had to do with being on the David Letterman show. To this day I have not tried to unravel that first dream. Another dream was about a wedding banquet. Now this is very curious to me as Jesus often used wedding banquets as images of what the kingdom of God is like. However, the dream I gave to Nancy was

21

the following:

"The Stump dream" Tuesday 8/23/94

At halftime of a football game there was this tree stump with an insect in it. He was green and he was fed another bug. I remember he grabbed it and held the other bug for a long time.

Nancy - How did you feel in the dream?
Me - I am not sure, but I kept thinking about it.
Nancy - Why do you think that is so?
Me - I just keep thinking about this green bug and what it was eating.
Nancy - What does halftime of a football game mean to you?
Me - Well, to me football is a rough but fun game. Sports are very important to me. I think football reflects life in many ways.
Nancy - How so?
Me - It is rough and tough and takes teamwork to get anywhere.
Nancy - That is a good analogy. So what is halftime?
Me - Halftime is a time to rejuvenate and replenish. It is a time to make adjustments.
Nancy - Maybe you are entering into a halftime?
Me - A time of rejuvenation?
Nancy - Yes. Do you think you need to make any adjustments in life?
Me - I should say so.
Nancy - What does a stump mean to you?
Me - I was thinking of Isaiah 11:1, where a shoot will come up from the stump of Jesse and a branch will bear fruit.
Nancy - So once again an image of rejuvenation.
Me - Yeah.
Nancy - What else is a stump?
Me - What is that book where the boy becomes an old man and sits on the tree stump that gave him everything?
Nancy - That's *The Giving Tree* by Shel Silverstein. The tree loved the boy so much it kept giving him what he needed throughout his life. Do you think God is inviting you to rest and be replenished?
Me - Maybe Jesus is the Giving Tree?
Nancy - Absolutely.
Me - I hope so.
Nancy - I know so.

22

Me - A stump is also simply a tree that has been cut down. Have I been cut down to start anew?
Nancy - Perhaps. What about this green insect?
Me - I think it was a plump caterpillar like insect.
Nancy - What do caterpillars do?
Me - Caterpillars go into cocoons to become butterflies.
Nancy - They need to eat to prepare for the transformation process, don't they?
Me - Yes, I would guess.

This dream was the first sip of water from that deep well. It was a powerful message to embrace. Now someone could have simply told me that God is going to support, rejuvenate, and transform me. However, there is something very powerful about knowing the message comes from God within you. God was alive, awake, active and moving inside of me. God was calling me to greater awareness or consciousness. Another dream I shared with Nancy early on was this:

"A storm is coming" Sunday 8/28/94

I dreamed I was at a park with my mom and brother. One of us was riding a red-type moped that was really nice. I looked up in the sky and the sky started to swirl. I looked again and the sky was dark. So I warned my mom and brother and they said ok in a nonchalant kind of way, and I remember wanting to place the red motor scooter in a safe place and I did, behind a shady tree. Then we took off down to a safe place. I was there on a porch and it seemed like everyone else was fully safe inside and not too concerned about the storm. I then thought there was going to be no storm because I could see only part of the sky and no one seemed concerned. Then I saw an Asian family coming to take shelter and she said it looks like there is going to be a storm. So I stepped off the porch and saw she was right. A storm was coming. Then I woke up.

Nancy - How did you feel in the dream?
Me - I felt confused, then relieved, and then I woke up very alarmed.
Nancy - What does a storm mean to you?
Me - Well, storms come along and blow things everywhere.
Nancy - They kind of rearrange things, huh?

23

Me - Yeah. Sometimes things get damaged.
Nancy - Sometimes. Sometimes things need to get damaged. What else do storms produce?
Me - Rain.
Nancy - And that does what?
Me - It helps things to grow.
Nancy - Right. So you think there is a storm brewing in your life?
Me - Yeah.
Nancy - I would say so. Things are never easy are they?
Me - Nope.
Nancy - Sometimes things get harder before they get better.
Me - How hard?
Nancy - Not too hard, but harder. Transformation thru inner work is definitely hard and rearranges our viewpoints in life, which can be scary. Although, even though a storm may seem scary, it is from God, and we will be renewed.
Me - We lose our innocent faith?
Nancy - Oh, yes. We all need to be cast out of the safe garden. What does a red moped or motor scooter represent for you?
Me - A moped to me is a fun toy to play around on to get from here to there. It is not a real motorcycle or car. It's kind of immature. You ride it when you are young.
Nancy - Maybe it means your boyish ways of getting around in the world are over. It's interesting. You are trying to protect it from the storm.
Me - But, I can't hide it though.
Nancy - How do you still do immature things?
Me - I don't know.
Nancy - Do you take care of all your finances, food, etc.?
Me - I am starting to.
   Nancy - Do you take it seriously?
Me - I guess.
Nancy - Maybe you should reflect on that. What about your mom and brother and the people in the house?
Me - Well, once again my mom and brother tie the scene to me being childish.
Nancy - Did your mother and brother take care of you when you were little?
Me - Sort of.
Nancy - They don't seem to be very helpful here.
Me - Nope.

Nancy - Maybe the storm is going to change how you rely on some things. They aren't useful to you anymore.

Reflection questions:
1. When have you felt dry in your life?
2. Who or what helped you through that time?
3. What helped you take that first step to the well of living water?

Chapter Four: The Power of Dreams

For God does speak—now one way, now another—though no one perceives it. In a dream, in a vision of the night, when deep sleep falls on people as they slumber in their beds, he may speak in their ears and terrify them with warnings, to turn them from wrongdoing and keep them from pride, to preserve them from the pit, their lives from perishing by the sword. (Job 33:14-18, NIV)

In the book of Job, young Elihu rebukes Job and his older three friends. They had been focusing solely on Job and whether he sinned or was righteous. Elihu instead rightly turns the focus to the righteousness of God. In Chapter 33 Elihu gives some great God-inspired wisdom about dreams. Elihu is not perfect in his advice to Job either, but he points out that God speaks to us through dreams. Further, he points out that God does so to inform us, keep us from doing wrong, and to keep us from pride. In fact, good dream analysis does all these things. Good dream analysis is prayerfully open to the wisdom of God. We are to be in dialogue with God about the dream and not too quick to judgment about what the dream means. Further, God informs us of what is going on in our souls (our psyche) through many symbols. This helps keep us from projections and thus wrongdoing. Finally, good God-focused dream analysis helps put us in our place and keep us from pride. It makes us aware of the grace of God. We do not do the work. God does the work. We are called to pay attention.

Practical advice on Dream Analysis

I am not a trained dream analyst, although I have learned certain important perspectives through twenty years in dream analysis that I will share. The most important thing is to pay attention, and hopefully discuss your dreams. One doesn't necessarily have to be a licensed analyst to get some meaning out of dreams. You simply need to have proper perspective and know the right questions to ask. Discussing your dreams in any way with another helps the unconscious know you are paying attention, at least in some way. However, to do in-depth dream analysis well, then you may need a trained dream analyst. Preferably one who also has a strong faith in God.

Nancy, my analyst or spiritual director as I called her, was a trained Jungian analyst. She studied for years at the Jungian Institute in Switzerland. She was also a strong Christian. Now I am not an expert on Jung, and I do not put him on a pedestal with the Holy Trinity, but I think he had a good way of looking at dreams. For a good summary of Jung's thought read *The Essential Jung* compiled by Anthony Storr, particularly the chapter on "The Practical Use of Dream-analysis." The following is at least the way I understand some of Jung's perspective. First, dreams give us a way of looking into the psyche. Psyche in Greek means soul.[4] Thus, dreams are windows into the soul. Second, dreams use symbol and you need to pay attention to the context of the dream because symbols can mean various things. Third, the psyche uses people and places that are real in our lives to direct us internally to deeper awareness and understanding.

Almost always, dreams are to make us aware of what is going on inside us. Dreams are thus tools to make us conscious of our inner life. This is part of the process Jung called Individuation or becoming conscious or psychologically whole. As a Christian priest I would say that it is a part of the process of becoming spiritually aware. Some would say it is to help us become fully human. We are called to be who God calls us to be, and awareness of who we are internally is a great part of that. Without being conscious of our inner life, we can unknowingly project and miss out on some great truths in our lives.

Further, dreams rarely predict the future. At least I know I have never had a dream in 22 years that did this. Although many of the dreams in the Bible predicted the future, and dreams can hint at events to come. Our unconscious can surely pick up on something that we may miss. All things are possible with God.

---

[4] Green and Robinson ed., *A Concise Lexicon to the Biblical Languages*, Greek 142.

So dreams could look to the future, but I do not believe that is generally their intent.

Dreams are more to be explored to teach us what is going on inside us now. They are like great inner paintings or works of art that trigger deeper thought and point toward truth. Once again, dreams can use people, places, and symbol to guide our journey. We have to ask ourselves what this person, place, or symbol means to us. That person, place, or thing represents an aspect of our inner being.

Here is something important to remember… our external life always prompts and informs our internal dream life, and the internal dream life always affects and influences the external life. The external informs the internal, and the internal influences the external. Jung talked about "assimilation" between conscious life and our unconscious life expressed in dreams.[5] Our unconscious will influence our lives whether we are conscious of it or not. It is obviously better to know what is going on inside our psyche. This is very important to keep in mind.

Another important aspect to point out is that the inner dream life does not give direct blueprints to fix our external lives. No, instead, dreams and our external lives go hand in hand informing one another so that by paying attention to both, we can grow more in the grace of God and be transformed along the way. Dreams do affect how we relate to the external world. However, it is more a process of growth and discovery than a fix-it. To do this we need to pay attention to how our dream ego (that is us in our dreams) relates to the people, places, and symbols.

People in our dreams represent an aspect of us. Thus, if you have a dream about someone else, then the important thing is to know how that person relates to you, and what characteristics they possess. Moreover, pay attention to what that person is doing in the dream. That part of us that person represents is changing and growing inside us. A person in a dream mirrors the external person, but the dream is not necessarily directly about that person. However, as you grow to understand this aspect of yourself internally, then it will affect your external relationship with that person as well.

Places are also very important. We need to know what a certain place means to us. Places give us great clues as to what the dream is teaching us. Sometimes, the unconscious uses a

---

[5] Jung and Storr ed., *The Essential Jung: Selected Writings*, 181.

place you do not know well. It is important to look up what that place is all about. For example, one time I dreamed about Piqua, Ohio. I knew very little about Piqua. However, my research led me to a story from the Shawnee Native Americans. They told the story of a man who came up out of the ashes. They exclaimed a phrase that included the word "Piqua" which means rising up out of the ashes.[6] This rising from the ashes was important to more fully understanding the dream.

The same is true of symbol. The first question to ask is, what does that symbol mean to you? From there we can explore and research the meaning of a specific symbol. Symbols can be negative or positive in our dreams (as can people and places). For example, a snake is often thought of as a negative symbol, one of temptation. However, a snake can also be a positive symbol of healing. You need to explore the symbols fully and how they are used in the dream to know what the dream may be telling you.

Dream Reflection Questions

Nancy always asked me similar questions each time we discussed a dream. **First, how did you feel in the dream?** The Holy Spirit often guides us to what is important through the aspects that emotionally stand out to us. This is also true of how we experience our external life as well. **Second, she would ask about important events in my external life the day of the dream.** Once again the external prompts and informs the internal, and the internal always influences the external whether we know it or not. In this book, as I look at my dreams, I do not go into the specific things affecting my life on the days I had the dreams. That would be way too much information, even though it is important to pay attention to how dreams relate to our current external lives. **Third, Nancy asked me to describe the people, places, and symbols in the dream.** Who are they to you? What do you associate with this place? Describe the symbols in your dream. What do they mean to you? **Finally, she would tell me to pay attention to one thing or another.** She might also challenge me in some way. I would always ask, "Do I need to do anything?" She would almost always say no. "You just need to become aware of what the dream is teaching."

---

[6] Rayner, *The First Century of Piqua, Ohio*, 10.

There is one more important thing to say about dreams. It is not important to pin down the exact meaning of a dream, but it is important to play with, explore, ponder, and see where they are guiding you. Dreams generally do not give us exact blueprints of what to do in our external lives. Dreams almost always tell us about who we are, and where we are in our spiritual lives. Thus, they are engines of change as we learn from and pay attention to them. In that way, dreams are one of God's ways of guiding us.

"The desire to get better" Wednesday 8/31/94

I was on a basketball team being coached by Reverend Ben. Then I went ahead and did one extra drill while the rest of the team lazily sat around. Then the coach made them do it (the extra drill) also. And I got to sit. I was glad that I motivated them. Then I realized that I was not allowed to sit while they did their drills, but why shouldn't I (sit). I then felt some tension and asked why they weren't working hard. One of them started bad mouthing the coach and I defended him (the coach). I gave a rah rah speech about how a coach can't create talent or motivate you if you don't want. You've got to want to get better.

Nancy - How did you feel during the dream?
Me - I am not sure.
Nancy - Well, you had to have some feeling.
Me - Do we always have feelings?
Nancy -Yes, we do...Perhaps you are not always aware of your feelings.
Me - Well, I guess I felt confused and excited.
Nancy - There you go. What does it mean to be on a basketball team?
Me - Well, basketball is my favorite sport. Playing basketball is when I truly let go and feel exhilarated.
Nancy - What does it mean to be on a team?
Me - Being on a team is important because we all need to help each other in life. In basketball you need your teammates on each play. Someone needs to throw the ball in. Someone needs to dribble it up the court. Someone needs to pick for you to get open. Someone tries to rebound when you miss a shot.
Nancy - So what are you doing in the dream?
Me - I am practicing with my team.

Nancy - Practice helps you get better, yes? So who are all these people?

Me - Well, I do not remember any of them specifically.

Nancy - in the dream they are lazy. Are you lazy?

Me - Sometimes.

Nancy - But you really want to get better?

Me - Yeah.

Nancy - But there is this conflict in the dream between you and some lazy people. Do you battle being lazy?

Me - Yes. At times. I can work really hard, and be very lazy at other times.

Nancy - Who is Reverend Ben?

Me - Reverend Ben is a priest I sought advice from last year.

Nancy - Did he give you good advice?

Me -Yeah.

Nancy - What did he tell you?

Me - He told me that it was normal to lose your childhood faith, and many people go through a dark night of the soul.

Nancy - Anything else?

Me - Yeah. He told me that he always found wisdom and relief in community.

Nancy - Do you struggle with that?

Me - With what?

Nancy - Community.

Me - Sometimes. I like to be alone.

Nancy - Are you alone too much, you think?

Me - Maybe.

Nancy - Maybe you should think about when you are lazy and avoid community, you think?

Me - Ok. Yeah, I guess. Is this a good dream?

Nancy - Well, you desire to get better, which is good.

Me - Do I need to do anything?

Nancy - No, just reflect on when and why you avoid community.

Reflection questions:
  1. How do you think God tries to connect with and teach you?
  2. Do you have any powerful dreams you remember?
  3. What people, places, and symbols might be important in your life?

Chapter Five: The Brokenness Within

One day as Jesus was standing by the Lake of Gennesaret, the people were crowding around him and listening to the word of God. He saw at the water's edge two boats, left there by the fishermen, who were washing their nets. He got into one of the boats, the one belonging to Simon, and asked him to put out a little from shore. Then he sat down and taught the people from the boat. When he had finished speaking, he said to Simon, "Put out into deep water, and let down the nets for a catch." Simon answered, "Master, we've worked hard all night and haven't caught anything. But because you say so, I will let down the nets." When they had done so, they caught such a large number of fish that their nets began to break. So they signaled their partners in the other boat to come and help them, and they came and filled both boats so full that they began to sink. When Simon Peter saw this, he fell at Jesus' knees and said, "Go away from me, Lord; I am a sinful man!" (Luke 5:1-8, NIV)

There are many scenes in the gospels where great crowds want to hear what Jesus says. I think this would be true today as well if Jesus was flesh and bones with us like he was in Galilee two thousand years ago. There is something charismatic about Jesus that naturally draws people to him. On some deep instinctual level we know he is full of wisdom. Even those who went away from Jesus thinking he was crazy, still would have to say there is something captivating about that Jesus.

I think we all realize that we are works in progress as human beings. We are not complete, whole, or even fully human the way we are intended to be. There is something missing in our souls. There is a hole in us that needs to be filled. Even the people who seem to have it all together are in the same boat. There are no perfect people.

Thus, we all ache to hear something that will change our lives. Something that will deeply satisfy us. "Hey, I hear this carpenter has some good things to say...let's go listen to him." This deep human yearning is why many times crowds grew up around Jesus.

A Deeper Invitation

As Jesus leaves the crowds he goes with Simon Peter into the deep waters. I love that phrase, and it has great meaning. Our souls are like deep waters, and we are called by God to go fishing with Jesus in them. Sadly not everybody moves from the crowd to inside the boat with Jesus to explore those deep waters. Many people in our world stay in the external and never explore the deep waters of the internal soul or psyche. Call it inner work or spiritual direction or individuation. It is paying attention to what goes on inside each of us.

We can do this in many ways. Most explore the inner by getting feedback from others. Some go deep in prayer and contemplation. Others pay attention to their unconscious material, which is mostly accessed through your dreams.

Peter must have thought Jesus was off his rocker. Here Peter, a seasoned fisherman, was taking orders from a carpenter. It makes me think of the fact that we all have great pride that gets in the way sometimes. Even though we all instinctively know we don't know everything, we still often refuse help or guidance. We think we are the experts. Will we really listen to and trust this Jesus? Sometimes we find the courage to check our pride at the door and listen to God in our lives. "Well, I guess I'll try...what do I have to lose," we say to ourselves.

Then out of nowhere all these fish come from the deep waters. Who knew there was so much down there? In fact, we are amazed there is anything at all in these deep waters. There are so many fish we cannot even pull them up on our own. This whole process is gift. We need the grace of God and the ability to trust.

Realizing what is in the deep

Peter tells Jesus to go away from him because he is a sinful man. We all become frightened when we realize something about ourselves that we never thought was there. When things come up out of the deep, our initial instinct is to think it will show us how bad we are. In fact, pulling up the fish from the deep is difficult, but not because it shows us how bad we are, but because it reminds us of how broken we are. We are all broken, you and me. When we are given the grace of God to pull up things from the deep it is scary at first, but it is the way to healing, to wholeness.

My first catch from the deep

In the fall of 1994, I was not aware of how broken I was. Oh, sure, I knew I was created good, and overall I was a good guy. I got along in society well, and generally people liked me. I also knew I was not perfect. I knew I was a sinner. Further, I knew there was something missing within, but what was it? Was I to blame for the darkness I was experiencing?

I always shrank from the word *sin*. I did not like to think that I did bad things. I certainly did not like being called a sinner. However, doing inner work with dreams transformed my understanding of sin. I read an incredibly enlightening chapter 3 in John Sanford's *Healing Body and Soul* about sin. I learned about a Greek word for sin, which is *hamartia*. The word literally means 'to miss the mark,' and comes from ancient words used by Greek archers. We can 'miss the mark' by doing bad things in our external life, or 'miss the mark' by missing what we are supposed to do according to God's law. Although there is another way of understanding this 'missing of the mark.' John Sanford writes, "A central Greek idea is that the inability of the archer to hit the target lies in a fault in the character or consciousness of the archer."[7] Thus, from an inner perspective sin is not focused on when we do bad things, but sin is the 'missing of the mark' in our souls due to lack of consciousness or awareness. Sin comes from those unaware parts inside of us that are hurt or broken or underdeveloped. This brokenness may lead us to sinful external actions. However, sinful actions are always rooted in the

[7] Sanford, *Healing Body and Soul*, 113.

35

inner. From this perspective on sin, the important thing to do is to get in touch with the inner hurt or brokenness.

Now I firmly believe that God created us in God's image and likeness. I do not believe that we are made bad. Instead our brokenness or 'missing of the marks' come from deep internal wounds. In fact, the moment we are born into creation we start internalizing and relating to a sinful and broken world that affects us. These 'missing of the marks' or internal wounds in our psyche are what God wants us to touch, to fish out. This is a painful process. We can say with Peter, "Go away from me, Lord; I am a sinful man!" (Luke 5:8) However, if we want to heal, if we want to explore our dreams and the unconscious, if we really want to fish those deep waters, then we need to go there with Jesus and explore that brokenness. If we do not, then we will unconsciously live out of that brokenness over and over and over again.

Inner wounds or 'missing of the marks' lead many to terrible things. We often wind up hurting ourselves and others. "What was the brokenness in me?" I wondered.

"The muddy pants" Thursday 9/1/94

I was leaving somewhere like college. I needed a ride home. I jumped in the back of this truck, I think I was with my brother and there was a good looking red-haired female. So when me and my brother jumped in the backseat I made sure I was sitting next to her. The guy driving us I recognized as some guy I met out west. In the dream I understood that he was always the guy who drove me to and from school. He had a friend in the front who was someone who was not overly bright. I remember he finally drove the route I wanted him to take. Like it was finally going to be done right. I showed my brother a few places where I had lived, but I could not point to them exactly. Then we made it to the driver's house and I jumped out of the truck and both the driver and I had on jeans that were really muddy. He was really mad and thought his folks were going to kill him. I just couldn't understand how mine (jeans) had gotten muddy. I remember seeing a small footprint from maybe like a small child on my pants. Then I got into a conversation with the guy in the passenger seat and I remember feeling empathy for him. Well, then the driver returned and was going to take me and my brother home. I decided to jump in the back seat of the pick-up. Then I remember my brother asked me if I had any money to pay the driver for gas.

36

He wouldn't accept a ten dollar bill from my brother thinking it was too much. I gave him a dollar bill and a lot of quarters. My brother offered me a cigarette and I felt really free.

Nancy - How did you feel in the dream?
Me - I felt anxious and angry at first, then I felt happy and free. I felt excited when I sat next to the red-haired girl.
Nancy - What do you think of when you think of a red-haired girl?
Me - I usually think of someone who is fiery, fun, and full of energy. I think of Ginger from *Gilligan's Island*. They are usually very attractive.
Nancy - And you are attracted to this girl in the dream?
Me - Yes. Very much so.
Nancy - And who is this driver?
Me - I recognized him as one of my bunk mates when I was out west in Yellowstone Park.
Nancy - Say more about him.
Me - When I was out West doing the program for the ministry in the National Parks, I stayed in a cabin with these real live cowboy ranch hands. We were at the most remote place in the park. These cowboys' job was to take groups out on a wagon ride, stop and cook steaks over the fire, and them tell funny cowboy stories to the people.
Nancy - Sounds like fun. They seem like fun-loving down-to-earth guys.
Me - Yeah, and a little off-the-wall and nutty too.
Nancy - And their driving your car?
Me - Yeah. What does that mean?
Nancy - A car often represents your ego. Someone driving your car in a dream is telling you who may be unconsciously steering you around. Looks like you have a nutty cowboy driving you right now. Do you feel crazy or out of control at times?
Me - Sometimes...probably.
Nancy - But he gets it right in the end. What about these muddy pants?
Me - I was going to ask you.
Nancy - What do you think they symbolize?
Me - Well, I would be embarrassed if I had muddy pants.
Nancy - Shame. What is your shame?
Me - I don't know. I guess I am ashamed I was a fraternity guy.
Nancy - How so?

Me - Well, I always felt like I lived a dual life. Sometimes as a Christian, sometimes as a fraternity guy.
Nancy - Did you do anything wrong?
Me - No, just stupid things.
Nancy - So you are ashamed of who you can be sometimes?
Me - I guess. Although I liked my fraternity.
Nancy - The dream doesn't indicate you did anything wrong, just that you feel shame.
Me - I guess there was nothing wrong partying.
Nancy - It is interesting there is a child's footprint on the muddy pants.
Me - Yeah.
Nancy - Could you feel shame as a child?
Me - Sure. I guess.
Nancy - I wonder where you picked up this inner shame?
Me - What?
Nancy - Well, the dream indicates you have this inner shame. It is like a 'missing of the mark.'
Me - A 'missing of the mark?'
Nancy - Yes. Sometimes we have inner hurts that affect our external actions. Something from your childhood made you internalize shame.
Me - Do I need to do anything?
Nancy - Maybe just reflect on where you picked up this shame. How do you describe your brother?
Me - My brother is closest to me in age. He is the person I was closest to while I was growing up. My brother thus knows about my childhood years the best. My brother is a very good guy who is very kind, but he is also deep down very intense.
Nancy - It is interesting. In the dream, your brother can't pay for you anymore.
Me - What does that mean?
Nancy - I am not sure, but definitely something to reflect on.

This dream started me on the journey to become aware of my brokenness, my 'missing of the marks,' my wounds, my sins. In the end of the dream my brother tried to pay for me, but I have to pay for this ride myself. Money often represents energy in dreams. I was being called to give my energy to get in touch with my inner brokenness. It is important to point out here that everybody has wounds from their childhood. The point is not to dwell on them, but to learn how they are affecting your present.

We are not to get stuck in blame of others if others hurt us. This does more damage than good. No, we are called to just identify the hurt and move forward. We are to own our brokenness, which means to be aware of it. This is always a painful process, but is essential in healing. The end result will be grace filled. Peter says, "Go away from me, Lord; I am a sinful man!" (Luke 5:8) We should all be so lucky to know our sinfulness as Peter did, and to be able to offer it to Jesus.

"My father going to the doctor" Saturday 9/3/94

I remember going to a doctor's office. I went with my dad. I wasn't sure why we were there. Then a nurse came out and called my dad to go back. He was the one who was sick.

Nancy - How did you feel in the dream?
Me - I felt confused, cold, and sad.
Nancy - What does it mean to be in a doctor's office?
Me - Well, of course you go to the doctor when you are sick. Who do you think is sick my dad or me? In the dream I thought my dad took me to the doctor. However, it was him who they called back.
Nancy - Interesting. Describe your Dad.
Me - My dad is a wonderful man. He is very hard working and caring. He is smart and very resourceful. He is a mechanical engineer by trade. He has been the director of quality assurance at a company in Dayton, Ohio, for over twenty years now. I use to joke with my dad. When he had a bad day I would say, "Well, you are a QA guy. You wouldn't have a job if everyone did everything perfect." My dad did not think I was funny. My dad could be a very stern man. He could get very mad. When he did I would avoid him. Dad was very particular about keeping his cars running and his yard in tip top shape.
Nancy - How does he deal with his emotions?
Me - As I say, my dad can get very mad, but he often broods and does not share his emotions. I know he felt withdrawn for some years while I was in middle school and early high school.
Nancy - How did that affect you?
Me - I guess it made me sad. We did not have the closest of relationships during that time. Although later in high school and in college dad was much better and more fun to be around. My dad was a jokester at heart and it finally came through.
Nancy - How are you like your father?

39

Me - Well, I can be pretty silly too. I am not near as meticulous as he is. I tend to bury my emotions as well, and can get very angry. I can also be very withdrawn.

Nancy - Can you think of a time when you buried your emotions?

Me - Well, this one time I remember as a young teenager getting very mad and passing out with anger.

Nancy - Oh, my goodness, that is awful.

Me - I do not remember the specifics of the argument, but I was standing on the step between the kitchen and the family room. My mom and dad were being condescending to me over something. I got very upset. I couldn't yell at them, but I ran up to my room and passed out with anger.

Nancy - Dan, that is very significant. Do you still bury your emotions?

Me - I guess I do.

Nancy - Can you go home and think of how and when you bury your emotions?

Me - I probably do it so often I don't even realize.

Nancy - This is very important stuff, a big internal wound in you. Now you know why you are at the doctor.

Me - It sucks being at the doctor. I hate it.

Nancy - Going to the doctor within is the way to healing.

Me - Jesus.

Nancy - Yes. Absolutely.

As I remember that time, I remember dealing with a lot of emotions. Below is an excerpt from my journal at that time:

I know the problem now. I don't and have never let people know me fully. I never report my feelings for what they are, but I analyze them first and then report them, then they stay that way inside me. I am sick of analyzing, but I know it will not go away right away, it will take time. I was always taught to suck it up and be good. But I also know that I don't condone or approve of people who act out every feeling or emotion they have. That can be too destructive as well. How do I find a balance?

One of my great 'missing of the marks' is that I would bury feelings. I would thus live this out unconsciously. Usually I would wind up only hurting myself, by feeling sorry for myself. Early in college I would drink myself into a stupor. Nancy suggested I read *The Artist Way* by Julia Cameron and do the morning pages she discusses in that book. The idea was to purge yourself of what was going on inside so you could be creative. For me, to journal was a way of getting in touch with my feelings.

Another word about people in our dreams

   I want to take this time to say a little more about people in our dreams. We often dream about people we know or famous people or people unknown to us but that have a distinctive characteristic like red hair. When we have anyone in our dreams, the first thing to remember is that the dream is not necessarily about that person. They are representing an aspect of you. You thus want to understand how you view the person, both good and not-so-good traits. We all have good and not-so-good traits. Pointing out someone's shortcomings does not mean that we love them less or that they are a bad person. No, it is simply how we experience them.
   We should also pay attention to the context of the dream. This helps define what aspects of their personalities the unconscious is trying to make known to us. It is also important to note that family and friends are very important in dreams.

Reflection questions:
   1. How do you understand sin?
   2. What brokenness in your psyche are you aware of?
   3. What helps you deal with your brokenness?

Chapter Six: Finding your Voice

"You are the light of the world. A town built on a hill cannot be hidden. Neither do people light a lamp and put it under a bowl. Instead they put it on its stand, and it gives light to everyone in the house. In the same way, let your light shine before others, that they may see your good deeds and glorify your Father in heaven." *(Matthew 5:14-16, NIV)*

"Let your light shine!" When I was in seminary, a few years after the events and dreams in this book, I had a wonderful priest mentor. His name is Reverend Chris and he was the priest of a church in Maryland. It is a beautiful old church located near the tip of Maryland where the Potomac River and Chesapeake Bay meet. There are some wonderful people who live down there in Saint Mary's County. This church was my field education placement. I went to train to be a parish priest. I would preach a little, teach a little, and learn a lot about rural parish ministry. Chris always said, "Dan, let your light shine." I think he knew I was tentative and not sharing all the gifts God had given me. I had heard this phrase before, "Let your light shine." I had read it not only in the Bible, but a few years earlier when Nancy encouraged me to "Get in touch with and find your voice."

Light the dark places

Jesus does not want us to be shy about sharing the God given gifts we have. Jesus says, "A town built on a hill cannot be hidden." (Matthew 5:14) Way before Ronald Reagan talked about America being a shining city on a hill, Jesus talked about it to inspire his followers. A town or city on a hill indeed cannot be hid. Often in ancient times cities were built on hills for defensive purposes, but also so that you could see them from miles around.

Cities on hills are impressive. Jesus wants the people of God to be a city on a hill, not to intimidate, but to be a shining example.

Jesus says the words at the beginning of this chapter as part of his sermon on the mount in Matthew's gospel. In this famous Sermon on the Mount, Jesus challenges us to go farther with our faith. Right before this he talks about being salt and light, and before that he gives the beatitudes. I often say that Jesus does not want us to realize how much God loves us, and then curl up in our beds and keep it to ourselves. No, if we have received the love of God, then we know it is a love that needs to be shared and shown to others. Be that impressive city on a hill that others see from miles away.

Jesus also uses the image of a lamp on a stand that gives light to the whole house. Nowadays we simply flip a switch when we enter a room and the whole room lights up. That was not so in Jesus' day. It was a challenge to light up a whole room or house. To light up a room, a lamp was strategically placed on a stand so that it could light up the entire room, or as much of it as possible. Lamps were there to bring light in the darkness, even in the remote corners of the room. Of course no one would light a lamp and put it under a bowl. What's the point of doing that?

So Jesus wants his followers to share their light, that is the light of the Holy Spirit in our lives. We do this by sharing our God-given gifts and the love of God. At the end of this passage Jesus reminds us of why we are to, "let your light shine before others." (Matthew 5:16) It is so they may see good works and give glory to God. How many people in the world see rotten works all around them? It is enough to make one want to curl up in bed and not share their God-given gifts with anyone. However, Jesus knows that the only way to combat the evil and tragedies of the world is to shine our lights. To do this well we need to find and share our God-given gifts, and to do this genuinely we need to connect with our inner voice.

Find that "inner" voice

We have all heard the phrase, "You need to find your voice." What does this mean? Well, a voice is a powerful thing. People often think of babies as helpless, until they spend a night with a newborn. Ask a brand-new parent who is the most powerful person in the house, and if they are wise they will say...the baby. A baby has the ability to get others to do things for them simply through using their voice. Newborns cannot walk, cannot crawl, cannot turn over, but they *can* use their voice.

We thus learn from an early age that we can affect things with our voices. Ask a teacher what the most important tool they have to manage their students and they will say their voice. I know many teachers, and they often talk about their teacher-voice. It just gets people to do things.

Voices are powerful. A great voice like Martin Luther King, Jr. can move the hearts of many. A madman like Adolf Hitler can bring great destruction. So it is a great responsibility having a voice. Singers use their voice to express themselves, to be creative. A voice can also express ideas and give power to people who are marginalized.

Further, you do not need to have a physical voice to share your gifts and power in the world. Once while in New York, I became very aware of how a taxi cab driver uses their voice. They use their car horns to express themselves and get others to move. In fact, using their horns is like an art. They can use it in many ways. They can of course give a loud sound to get others out of their way, but they often tap their horns to acknowledge others and let others know they are there. There is a whole horn language I never knew existed. I came from the passive aggressive Midwest where car horns are rarely used, at least where I lived.

People can express themselves in many ways. People play instruments, draw pictures, paint paintings, sculpt, work in wood, design landscapes, write books, etc. Thus, to use your voice is to express yourself, and to find your voice is to get in touch with God-given gifts and your inner self. This voice is what you are called to share and express.

Finding your Voice is about finding your identity and gifts, but we also need to take it one step further. It is also about expressing your true presence and authority in the world. As a Christian we know that finding our true voice comes from God. It is a process. Jesus reminds us always to, "Let your light shine." (Matthew 5:16)

A life-long work

I believe that it is a lifelong process to find your identity and your voice. Not that we are false throughout life. No, we can genuinely be in touch with our identity and voice. However, we never fully get in touch with our whole identity and our full voice.

We never graduate from life. It is always process. There is actually joy found when we realize we are always a work in progress. We can find that paying attention to the process is more important and satisfying than thinking we have reached our goal and are now done.

Another important aspect to know about inner voices is that sometimes we can be completely out of touch with ours. Some people can be seriously out of touch with who they are and with how they express their voice in the world. Many times people get caught up in self-interest and greed. Sometimes people buy into something that is very destructive. In other instances people can become so deceived that it is very difficult to connect with their true voice. People can have a glimpse of their identity and voice, but be too afraid to share it. They may be afraid it may turn them into someone they are not, or that sharing their voice may put them outside of a group they overly and falsely value.

Focus on Christ's sacrificial love

As a Christian, I believe that our identity and voice are found when we focus on the sacrificial love of God through Jesus Christ. Jesus says, "For whoever wants to save their life will lose it, but whoever loses their life for me will save it." (Luke 9:24) This statement seems contradictory, but it is actually full of truth. When we let go of our self-interests replacing them with the love of God and others, then we truly find our identity and voice. I often say that when our focus is "me, me", then we are lost. However, if our focus is on the other and God, then we find God, the other, and ourselves. From this identity we can share our voice.

This finding of our identity and voice is an internal process as well. To let go of self-interests and to love others and God, we need to look at how God is guiding us internally. Thus, to let go of our self-centeredness, we need to look deeper within ourselves. Once again this seems contradictory at first, but it is not.

My voice quest

In 1994 I was not fully connected to my true voice. In truth I had just scratched the surface. I thought I knew myself well, but God was to show me much more. Now this does not mean I was completely disconnected from my identity and voice, but I certainly was swimming to find myself. I think many of us go through this process. We wake up one day and we realize something glaring is missing.

For me at this time, I was transitioning from college to the so called "real world." In the recent past I had found a lot of my identity in being a leader in my fraternity house. I was also still very connected to the church. In college I very much lived a dual life, fraternity guy/Christian. I actually took both very seriously. I was a leader in my fraternity and genuinely wanted to help the guys in the house. They were good guys, and I felt good about myself drawing my identity from the fraternity. I also took my Christian faith seriously. I served as a youth minister at a church in a rough neighborhood in Columbus. I helped as a counselor at our Diocesan church summer camps. Bridging these two worlds seemed difficult at times. I would often hide my Bible in the fraternity house, and I would shy away from letting others at church know who I was as a fraternity guy.

After my college days were over, I was going through a process of discovering my identity apart from these groups of people. I think we always gain a piece of our identity and voice from our relationships. We are in fact relational beings. However, if we can only identify ourselves by the groups we are in, then we will never find our true identity and voice. As we mature we are called to find our identity and voice as individuals connected to groups and in relationship, but not our total identity wrapped up in a group. Sometimes we have to leave the group to uniquely identify ourselves, and then later we are able to reconnect with others in more mature relationships. This is what I was experiencing in 1994, and it was painful.

Also, I needed to more fully connect with my emotions. This would be a constant theme for me. I had been taught so often to keep my emotions in check, and even to squash them. It made it very difficult to connect with my true inner self. We need to know what we feel, to know our true identity and to express our voice. I had learned so well to keep my emotions in check, that I would often completely dismiss my feelings not even knowing they were there. This is an extreme detriment to finding your voice. It is impossible to be who you truly are in relationship with people when you do not even know how you are feeling. I would be wearing a mask around others and did not even know it.

In addition to this I was struggling with my faith. Now I had always said that, "If you can't test your faith, then how can it become stronger?" This of course comes from similar sayings in the Bible like, "Consider it pure joy, my brothers and sisters, whenever you face trials of many kinds, because you know that the testing of your faith produces perseverance." (James 1:2, 3) However, it is easier to say this, than to go through it. It became very clear to me that a huge part of my voice was going to be tied to my faith, even in times of struggle. My feet kept taking me to places to explore my faith. They took me to churches and Bible study groups. They took me to prayer services and people to discuss my faith. Finding my true voice, and letting my light shine as a Christian were always going to be intertwined.

"Celebrating and speaking God's words" - Monday 8/29/94

I was up at the altar with all these important ministers. I was sitting there in an acolyte position. Then I left during the sermon and was pushing something around, I can't remember what. And the sermon was short, so I was late getting back to church. Then during the Eucharist, all the parishioners were kneeling, and two very distinguished Bishops were to the left. Everybody was kind of talking while Rev. Steve was trying to say the Eucharistic prayer. So I just got so mad and stopped everything and yelled at all of them, and told them I thought they stunk and I left. Afterword I talked to Rev. Steve who was lying on the floor in front of the altar totally distressed and I gave him advice.

Nancy: How did you feel in the dream?
Me: I was anxious and upset.
Nancy: Say more about that.
Me: I felt anxious when I missed the sermon, and I felt angry when no one would listen to Steve.
Nancy: What does it mean to be an acolyte?
Me: I have been an acolyte since I was in fourth grade. My oldest brother trained me to be an acolyte. I have always loved to be an acolyte, to be around the altar. Acolyting is when you help the priests with the sacraments.
Nancy: So that is very important to you?
Me: It has been.
Nancy: You feel at home near the altar?
Me: Yes
Nancy: Do you like listening to sermons? What do you learn?
Me: I have learned to listen to sermons as I have gotten older.

48

Nancy: Do you remember any specific sermons.

Me: Not off the top of my head. I like to hear about how God relates in my life. One of my favorite books of late is Frederick Buechner's *The Magnificent Defeat*. It is a book of his sermons on God's love claiming your life.

Nancy: But in the dream you miss the sermon or the message because you are pushing something around right?

Me: Yes.

Nancy: Do you think you miss the message that God loves you?

Me: Maybe. I mean I know it…

Nancy: But do you know it in your heart?

   (Silence)

Nancy: What about these important ministers and Bishops, who are they?

Me: I can't remember any of them specifically; I mean none of them was someone I knew in my life.

Nancy: But they were important figures in the dream, right? What does a Bishop represent to you?

Me: They are defenders of the faith.

Nancy: But here they are talking while Steve is trying to celebrate the Eucharist?

Me: Yep.

Nancy: Do you think you have trouble connecting with your inner authority? I mean, do you find it hard to give your voice on some matters?

Me: Maybe sometimes.

Nancy: Especially to important people, right?

Me: I guess.

Nancy: And who is Steve?

Me: Steve is a young priest in the diocese. He is the director of youth ministries for the diocese.

Nancy: Do you like Steve? Describe him? Does he have trouble expressing himself?

Me: Oh, no. He is a great guy. I like him a lot. He is always excited and has lots of ideas. He is also very obnoxious and funny.

Nancy: So he doesn't have trouble expressing himself. Is there a part of you like him? A part of you who gets excited and has ideas?

Me: Yes.

Nancy: Do you share it?

Me: Sometimes.

49

Nancy: Well, here in the dream your young vibrant voice is being drowned out by others, specifically authority figures. You want to hear Steve, but you can't, and you get upset about it.
Me: Yes.
Nancy: And then you console Steve and give him advice. Do you give Steve advice in your external life?
Me: Generally no.
Nancy: But here you are. I think perhaps you really want this part of you that Steve represents, this young, vibrant figure that celebrates even in front of authority to come out, eh? You want to find and express that voice in you, yes?
Me: Yes. I guess so.
Nancy: You guess so?
Me: I mean yes. Definitely. Do I need to do anything?
Nancy: No, just keep paying attention to your dreams, maybe journal about your inner voice, and pay attention to when you want to share something from deep inside you.

"Lost at a speech tournament" Wednesday 11/9/94.

I was at a speech tournament and I ran into my speech coach. I had a new speech that was going to be very good and I wanted to make the cut. I told my speech coach that I really wanted to do well. First round I was late and the judge wouldn't let me in to give my speech. I was really mad. I knew I could have been the best in the round. The next round I screwed around trying to find a place to practice. Then I got up to go and could not remember my lines at all. I knew if somebody could just prompt me I would be fine. I wound up losing that round too. But I was determined to remember the speech and do well tomorrow for the final rounds.

Nancy: How did you feel in the dream?
Me: I felt anxious, but excited.
Nancy: You also ended the dream determined, right?
Me: Yes. Definitely.
Nancy: Have you ever been to a speech tournament?
Me: Yes.
Nancy: What is it like?
Me: I have been in many speech tournaments. I was on the speech team in high school.
Nancy: Did you enjoy them?

Me: Sometimes. I usually did humorous interpretation, or duet acting or something like that. I never did very well in speech tournaments.

Nancy: Who is your speech coach? Did she help you?

Me: Oh, yes. She was very good. She always believed in me. She always thought I could do better than I did.

Nancy: It feels good to have someone encourage and believe in you.

Me: Yes, it does, absolutely.

Nancy: In the dream you think you can be pretty successful with your new speech.

Me: Right.

Nancy: Do you notice you have a new speech or voice in life?

Me: I think so...maybe...I am not sure.

Nancy: What might that be?

Me: Well, all of this inner work I am learning, and how it relates to the Church and the Bible.

Nancy: But you miss some opportunities to share your new speech because you are late or you need more time to practice?

Me: Yes.

Nancy: That would be frustrating.

Me: Yes, it would. Do I need to be doing anything more?

Nancy: No, you just need to keep paying attention...Your voice is coming along.

Reflection questions:
1. What do you think your gifts are? How do you share them?
2. What keeps you from letting your true light shine?
3. What are some things emerging inside you now? Are you learning to express these new gifts?

Chapter Seven: Take a Walk on the Wild side

In those days John the Baptist came, preaching in the wilderness of Judea and saying, "Repent, for the kingdom of heaven has come near." This is he who was spoken of through the prophet Isaiah: "A voice of one calling in the wilderness, 'Prepare the way for the Lord, make straight paths for him.'" John's clothes were made of camel's hair, and he had a leather belt around his waist. His food was locusts and wild honey. People went out to him from Jerusalem and all Judea and the whole region of the Jordan. Confessing their sins, they were baptized by him in the Jordan River. But when he saw many of the Pharisees and Sadducees coming to where he was baptizing, he said to them: "You brood of vipers! Who warned you to flee from the coming wrath? Produce fruit in keeping with repentance. And do not think you can say to yourselves, 'We have Abraham as our father.' I tell you that out of these stones God can raise up children for Abraham. The ax is already at the root of the trees, and every tree that does not produce good fruit will be cut down and thrown into the fire. I baptize you with water for repentance. But after me comes one who is more powerful than I, whose sandals I am not worthy to carry. He will baptize you with the Holy Spirit and fire. His winnowing fork is in his hand, and he will clear his threshing floor, gathering his wheat into the barn and burning up the chaff with unquenchable fire." (Matthew 3:1-12, NIV)

All four gospels begin Jesus' ministry with his encounter with a hairy wild man named John the Baptist. John is often referred to as the last and greatest of the prophets. In many ways he is the quintessential man of God, and we can all learn from him.   In the church year we encounter this wild prophet dripping with water every second Sunday of Advent. In advent we are called to reflect on Christ's arrival or coming. We are made aware that the Jewish people went through a time of waiting for the messiah, and that we too are in a waiting period. We are waiting for Christ to come again. So we go back to Jesus' baptism which binds us all together. We are reminded that Jesus was baptized by a hairy, wild, righteous man named John.

There is much to this scene, and I will only focus here on a few aspects. First, we must be aware of what John was doing. He was fulfilling the words of the prophet Isaiah to prepare a way and make our paths straight. John was preaching a baptism of repentance for the forgiveness of sins. Now Jews knew all about ritual bathing. It was very central to many of their lives. In the Torah, whenever someone erred or had something happen to make them ritually unclean, they were required to go and become ritually cleansed. Many Jews of Jesus' day used something called a *mikveh* or ritual bath.[8] The basic concept was that whenever you did something that made you ritually unclean you needed to be cleansed. You did this multiple times as needed. This would keep you as clean as one can be in the presence of God.

John, however, was talking about something a little different. John was talking about a one-time baptism for the repentance of sins. It was a way of marking a new life. We have already discussed in chapter five the meaning of sin. Here the word repentance is key. For many Christians, repentance is something we do whenever we mess up. We often think of repenting, especially when we do something really bad. We think we need to get right with the Lord again, and turn back to God.

This is not how John the Baptist understood repentance. For John, repentance is not turning back, but turning forward. Here the Greek word for repentance is *metanoia*. Literally *meta* means "change" or "beyond" and *noia* comes from the Greek *nous* for "mind". Thus *metanoia* or repentance is "a change of" or "to go beyond" one's mind or understanding.[9] It is a change of one's mind toward the world or a turning forward to a new understanding in life. Specifically, a turning forward to a new understanding of God's kingdom, which is love, mercy, and sacrifice. This is more powerful than just saying you are sorry so you can go back to the way things were before. No, in all we do, even when we sin, we

---

[8] Dosick, *Living Judaism: The complete guide to Jewish Belief, Tradition, and Practice*, 260.

[9] Childress and Macquarrie ed., *The Westminster Dictionary of Christian Ethics*, 535.

can learn anew, and go beyond our current understanding. Repentance is thus always striving forward to a new way of living. For John the Baptist, baptism marks this new life of repentance.

Another thing to point out about John the Baptist is his great connection with nature. He was wild, and not in a bad way. Being a wild man can be good, very good. It is written that he wore clothes of camel's hair, wore a leather belt, and ate locusts and honey. That is, he is far from a well-dressed politician or someone who feasted sumptuously from a banquet table every night. No, John the Baptist was greatly connected to nature and to God through his earthiness. He was wild.

There is a different consciousness when we are directly connected to God through nature. Sadly now we are conscious to our coffee makers, cell phones, cars, and televisions. We lose out on the basic connection of God through nature. We lose our wildness. John did not have that problem.

I do not know about you, but I grew up a suburban brat with most of the modern comforts. However, I always loved camping out or spending a week with my Grandma in West Virginia, because it slowed me down. It helped me to focus on what really matters in life. Connecting with the great outdoors helps one focus on a direct dependence and relationship with God through creation. We often strive in society to live more and more comfortably which is further and further away from God in nature. However, I think deep down we have a desire to connect with our wild side.

A third aspect of this story of John the Baptist is his righteous, honest, anger towards the Pharisees and Sadducees. John yells at them,"You brood of vipers! Who warned you to flee from the coming wrath?" (Matthew 3:7) John would probably not do well as a church greeter.

The Pharisees and Sadducees are interesting people. They are two of the prominent sects of Jewish people in John and Jesus' day.[10] Many of whom thought of themselves as very righteous. Please note that in the gospels when Jesus or John call out the Pharisees, Sadducees, or other Jewish groups of people, they are not condemning them all as awful people doomed to hell. Jewish people, or any group of Jewish people, should never be condemned as a result of incidents portrayed in

---

[10] Brown, *An Introduction to the New Testament*, 76,77.

the gospels. Jesus never condemns whole groups of people nor hates certain Jewish groups of people. However, certain groups of Jewish people are sometimes pointed out as often having people who pay more attention to the literal meaning of scripture rather than the heart beneath the words of scripture. There are people like this in every religious tradition. Jesus and John, being Jewish, just happen to be in contact with many self-righteous people in the Jewish world. The Pharisees and Sadducees knew all the Jewish laws and traditions. They took great pride in following their understanding of God's laws. They dotted their religious "i's" and crossed their "t's". Thus, later in the gospels they had many encounters and sharp conflicts with Jesus over issues like dietary and Sabbath laws. You could say that many of them were the ancient equivalent of a modern-day Bible thumper who knows every tradition and scripture passage and points out how everyone else is wrong. Some of them thus miss the great message of love, mercy, and forgiveness that God is truly teaching. This is the reason for the conflict, not because they identified themselves as Pharisees, Sadducees, or any other group of Jewish people.

John the Baptist, like Jesus, could see right through their hypocrisy. Not many others could. God's law was external for the Pharisees and Sadducees. They were rules you had to follow, and not a matter of the heart. John the Baptist, though, was called by God to preach about a change of mind, which was also a change of heart.

Further, John saw through their misguided understanding that they were chosen by God because it was their birthright. "Do not think you can say to yourselves, 'We have Abraham as our father.'" (Matthew 3:9) John the Baptist knew it was one's heart, not heritage, that mattered to God. This misguided and dangerous thinking still leads to great tragedies and wars in the world today.

Finally, John the Baptist was a great man of God because he pointed beyond himself to Jesus. He knew that, "But after me comes one who is more powerful than I, whose sandals I am not worthy to carry. He will baptize you with the Holy Spirit and fire." (Matthew 3:11) A true wild man of God does not point to themselves or live for themselves. They live for a loving God. They point to Jesus who represents sacrificial love.

I believe there are four possible foci in life. First we can be focused on self. We can make "me, me" the most important thing in life, looking out only for number one. This focus in life will always fail us. Second, we can be focused on another. We can be so in love with another person that they are the only thing that matters. Our whole identity is caught up in that person. This is good in the sense that we are looking beyond ourselves, but that other person is human, too. They are not perfect and will surely fail and disappoint us at some point. Third, we can be focused on an object of desire. We can get so caught up and obsessed about a thing or possession that we lose all perspective on the rest of life. Whether it is searching for the holy grail or trying to have the biggest house, chasing after and making objects our gods only leads to disappointment. However, a fourth focus in life can be God. Which for me is focus on Jesus Christ, which is focus on sacrificial love. When we have this as our focus, then self, others, and objects all find their proper place. John the Baptist was a true wild man of God who focused on and pointed to Jesus.

My distant wild man within

In the fall of 1994, I wasn't sure what it meant to be a real man, or a real man of God, let alone a wild man of God. I was twenty-three years old and searching in this incredible time of immense doubts to find what it meant to be a man of God. I remember the Dean of the cathedral pulling me into his office around this time and telling me, "You are your own man now, Dan." What did that mean I wondered? I thought back to a Led Zeppelin song *Good Times, Bad Times* which begins by saying, "In the days of my youth I was told what it means to be a man, now I've reached that age I try to do all those things the best I can."[11]

What did I learn about being a man? Was I really a man? Young boys are always taught how important it is to grow up and be a real man. What was that? I had heard my friends talk about being a man of God. What was that? How could I be a man of God when I intensely doubted the existence of a loving, caring God?

---

[11] Led Zeppelin, "Good Times / Bad Times," track 1 on *Led Zeppelin*, Atlantic, 1968.

Different models of manhood

I think the earliest lesson I learned about being a man is that all men should be in control of their emotions. This is the famous "real men don't cry" saying that truly winds up hurting all men. My brothers reinforced this as I would be called a cry baby if I ever did let loose a sniffle. As a result I learned not to cry but to be tough. Whenever I was tough it was rewarded. "Good job, little Layden," was what I was told when I was tough and played football or basketball with the older kids. I ate that up, and it is good to be tough. However, it is not good to always stifle your tears and to try to be in control of all your emotions all the time. My dad was generally in control of his emotions except when he would curse in the garage trying to fix the car or yell at the TV when his team would lose. Sadly, these are two behaviors that I can still display. The damaging aspect of always being in control is when it is done at the expense of important emotions you need not control.

This model to always be in control was unrealistically reinforced by male characters on TV. My favorite TV heroes were Captain James T. Kirk of *Star Trek*, Adam West of the *Wild, Wild West*, and Steve Austin the *Six Million Dollar Man*. I wanted to be like them. They were always in control, never cried, and always won in the end.

Another model for being a man emerged as I grew older. This was the image of a macho man or daredevil. This was someone who always craved adventure and would do crazy things to the applause of many. Evel Knievel was the great daredevil of my childhood. He was a macho guy who rode his motorcycle over the Grand Canyon. What a manly thing to do!? I had an Evel Knievel action figure with a motorcycle you could rev-up and run across the floor. There was also the manly, macho Fonz on *Happy Days*. He too jumped things on his motorcycle, and he got all the ladies at the snap of his finger. "Surely that is a real man," I would think. The macho/daredevil type image is always there for young boys. Once again, macho/daredevil men never cry even when they are lying in traction at a hospital. They are tough guys. In many ways all boys are taught to be cool and macho. Overall, I was a pretty fearless kid, a daredevil on a much smaller scale. My friends and I would jump bikes, ride dirt bikes, mopeds, and motorcycles, climb way up in trees, and scream on roller coasters. Unfortunately, I just couldn't snap my fingers and have the girls come running.

Another manly image that was central to my identity growing up was the sports man. Now this is important to many boys. We are taught toughness, fairness, and competitiveness. Once again these are not bad things. In fact in some ways the athletic arena was where we could express ourselves, be aggressive and assertive, and be praised. The sportsman was also very celebrated. People like Michael Jordan and Lawrence Taylor were the idols of millions. Many of us were taught, "Winning is not the most important thing, it is the only thing." I was much more of a sporto than anything else. I spent hours and hours on the basketball court, on the baseball field, and playing backyard football. There are a lot of great lessons one can learn in sports like teamwork and hard work. The shortfall is that all life and being a man is not about competition or beating the other guy. The sports arena is not the only place a man can be wild and show passion.

Another image of a man is the comedic man or funny guy. A real man knows how to have fun. Great comedic men like Eddie Murphy, Steve Martin, Chevy Chase, and Bill Murray knew how to get a laugh. Real men had a sense of being funny and knowing how to express themselves using vulgar language. Now my friends and I thought we were funny guys. We knew how to be class clowns and get much attention. To this day I do not know how my middle school teachers put up with us. We would often receive lunch detentions and as a result were put in corners of the lunchroom. Now that's smart, give the class clowns a free stage in front of everyone. Like the other models of being a man, the comedic man is not all bad. In fact, it is very important to laugh and be able to laugh at oneself. Sadly, though, we can learn to hide behind humor and not really have to express our true selves and feelings.

The civilized man is yet another image of masculinity. Here we are taught that once again a real man is always in control, dresses nicely for success, and is always polite. My dad always wore a tie and dressed up for important occasions. He taught me how to tie a tie, open doors for ladies, and say please and thank you. Later, in my fraternity days, we were taught how to act at formal dinners and to be a real man on a date (while at the same time being out of control party animals that drank too much, burned couches, and jumped on the hood of our cars). Once again the civilized man is not a completely bad model. It is wonderful to be polite and be nicely dressed. As ZZ Top boldly sings, "Everybody's crazy 'bout a sharp dressed man."[12] However, we can get trapped in this model behind looking good and being courteous, and not be connected to our natural selves.

Finally, as a Christian I was taught to be a sensitive man. Through youth groups and camps I was in many ways taught to reconnect to the sensitive side that was squelched by the macho/sports/comedic/civilized man. In our culture during the 80's and 90's many men were connecting with their sensitive side. It is a wonderful and freeing thing to learn to cry and be honest with your sensitive feelings. For me as a late teen and early twenty-something, it was a revelation that many girls liked sensitivity (at least the ones I often met in church circles). I learned to share and be vulnerable. Further, I certainly did not become only the sensitive man. I still was the sporto, clown, and sometimes civilized man. The biggest drawback to masculine development in the sensitive man model is that, yes, you can connect with some emotions of caring, sadness, and vulnerability, but what you still squelch is assertiveness, aggression, and righteous anger. These remain bottled up. They are bottled up because they can be scary. To truly connect with them can make us feel like we will be out of control and perhaps hurt others. Good Christians do not do this, do they? Weren't all the disciples choir boys? My dreams and Nancy introduced me to the wild man, which is a way of connecting with some natural life giving energy.

A real man to me is a little of all the models I have just given, but a real man also needs to connect with the wild man within. A true man for me is one who can connect with their true nature, inner identity, feelings, and learn to express them well. As human beings we are never going to be perfect at this, but we can always be in process to deepen our identity.

True Manhood versus Masculinity

There is a difference between being a real man and being masculine. As I wrote above, to be a real man I believe we are called to connect with all aspects of our nature, inner being, feelings, and learn to express them. This means connecting with and knowing our past. It means embracing our feminine side

---

[12] ZZ Top, "Sharp Dressed Man," track 3 on *Eliminator*, Warner Bros., 1983.

(which will be discussed in later chapters). Finally it means to connect with our inner wild man who has masculine traits. For me there are differences between masculine and feminine traits, and everyone is made up of masculine and feminine traits. Femininity is nurturing, caring, sustaining. Masculinity is assertive, aggressive, protecting. Notice I did not say women are *only* nurturing, caring, sustaining and men are *only* assertive, aggressive, protecting. Men and women each have a feminine and masculine side. Granted most women are more in touch with their femininity, but they can also be aggressive, assertive, or protecting. At the same time, men tend to be more masculine, but also have feminine traits. The goal is to be a whole human. It is to learn to embrace all our inner characteristics.

To finally touch the wild side

For me, though, in 1994, I had squelched the wild man masculine within. I was not in touch in a healthy way with aggression, assertiveness, and righteous anger. John the Baptist was one of the last people I would identify with in the Bible at the time. However, after the dream I will share next, Nancy encouraged me to read Robert Bly's book *Iron John* which talks about the need for men to connect with wild man energy. To get in touch with this I was encouraged to healthfully explore my anger, pay attention to when I shied away from being assertive, and to reflect on ways to be aggressive in positive ways outside of sports. I learned that being a wild man in relationships was important.

For me to tap into that energy, I spent time on walks screaming out to God and whacking a stick against the ground or a tree. I do not condone violence or breaking things, but there is something cleansing about being outside, shouting out, and being physical when it doesn't hurt anyone or destroy things. This and dream analysis and reflection helped me learn to not be afraid of such emotions. I was not hurting anyone; I was getting more fully in touch with my wild man masculine, life-giving energy.

"The wild man basketball player." Thursday 9/8/94.

I was playing basketball for Indiana and we were really playing bad. We were playing girls and should be killing them. Then someone made two free throws for the other team and tied the game. Then the ball went out of bounds and nobody wanted or seemed to want to play again except Ted and I. The coach asked who wanted to take the ball out and I said, "I do." Then I realized that Ted was the better man for the job.

Nancy: How did you feel in the dream?
Me: I was angry and then sad at the end.
Nancy: Why were you sad?
Me: Because I realized that Ted was the better man for the job.
Nancy: Let me start from the beginning. So you are playing basketball for Indiana?
Me: Right.
Nancy: What does that mean to you?
Me: Well, coach Bob Knight is the coach at Indiana, and they take basketball very seriously.
Nancy: Isn't he the coach who gets very emotional?
Me: Yes.
Nancy: Do you get upset easily?
Me: Yes, sometimes.
Nancy: But you have trouble expressing that anger.
Me: Yes, but not on the basketball floor.
Nancy: There you let it all hang out.
Me: Yep.
Nancy: That's interesting. Why do you think you hold back in life, but not on the basketball floor?
Me: I guess I was taught that it was okay to be emotional in sports…
Nancy: But not in real life.
Me: Yes.
Nancy: It is interesting that you are playing girls here.
Me: Yeah.
Nancy: Have you ever played basketball against girls?
Me: Very rarely. Only a few times.
Nancy: Is it different playing girls?
Me: Yeah, I would say so.
Nancy: Why?
Me: I don't know…I guess I feel like I can't be as aggressive.
Nancy: I wonder where you picked that up. Are you assertive when you are around girls off the basketball floor?
Me: No…no way.
Nancy: Why? Are you afraid?

Me: I don't know if I am afraid.

Nancy: But you are afraid, you are afraid to be too aggressive right?

Me: I guess so.

Nancy: You guess so? Is it wrong to be assertive and aggressive?

Me: I don't know. I guess sometimes it is alright.

Nancy: Can you share your aggression and assertiveness in a healthy way, or is it better to stifle that energy?

Me: I guess I need to learn to share and be more assertive.

Nancy: Who is Ted?

Me: Ted is a friend of mine I grew up with.

Nancy: Describe him.

Me: Well, he is a great guy, one of my best friends. I have known him my whole life. He is a very emotional guy.

Nancy: In a good way or a bad way?

Me: Mostly a good way.

Nancy: Is he assertive?

Me - Can be.

Nancy - Is he assertive around girls?

Me: Oh, yes. Much more than I am.

Nancy: Have you read the book *Iron John*, by Robert Bly?

Me: No.

Nancy: You should read it. It talks about men getting in touch with their wild nature or side.

Me: Okay. Is there anything else I need to do?

Nancy: Just pay attention to your deep emotions and find a way to express them.

Me: Like how?

Nancy: Write or draw out your feelings. Get outside, go for a walk or hike and think about your deep emotions. Find a place where you can shout out.

Me: Ok.

Reflection questions:
1. What does it mean to you to be a true man or true woman?
2. How are you connected to your wild side? How are you overly connected to the modern comforts of the world?
3. How do you think you can get more in touch with your wild energy?

Chapter Eight: Jesus hugs our inner child

They came to Capernaum. When he was in the house, he asked them, "What were you arguing about on the road?" But they kept quiet because on the way they had argued about who was the greatest. Sitting down, Jesus called the Twelve and said, "Anyone who wants to be first must be the very last, and the servant of all." He took a little child whom he placed among them. Taking the child in his arms, he said to them, "Whoever welcomes one of these little children in my name welcomes me; and whoever welcomes me does not welcome me but the one who sent me." (Mark 9:33-37, NIV)

Who is the greatest? Well, the greatest what? Runner? Boxer? Artist? Singer? Etc? Muhammad Ali did not hesitate when he yelled out, "I am the greatest. I float like a butterfly and sting like a bee." We have all argued about who is the greatest of something or other. People love a good countdown. At the end of the last century ESPN did a countdown of the *Top 50 American Athletes of the Twentieth Century.* People who love that sort of thing got in great arguments over whether Michael Jordan, Babe Ruth or Muhammed Ali was the greatest. ESPN had polled some experts and they were asked to rank each athlete's greatness by their impact on the sports world, championships, and dominance in their respective sports. Of course it is all based largely on opinion, but sports fanatics love to argue about these things. So, also, in other walks of life, people love to argue about greatness. We like to rank and debate who is the best.

Heck, even the disciples want to know who is the greatest among them. In fact they feel they need to know, and they need to know now because they are not sure how long Jesus may be around. After all, this argument about who is the greatest takes place right after Jesus gives what scholars call a passion prediction. He tells them the son of man will be betrayed and killed and three days later rise again. Now I am pretty sure the disciples did not fully understand what Jesus is predicting. However, I do think they know he is talking about betrayal and death. The disciples must have wondered, "When Jesus says, 'The son of man is to be...' does he mean himself?" At any rate Jesus is talking about death and betrayal.

As a result of Jesus' predictions, the disciples need to know who is the greatest in their group. That is, who can lead them if Jesus does die? I would guess they talked about which one of them was the strongest, or the best speaker, or the best teacher, or who had the greatest faith. They need to know who is the best to lead them.

Jesus knows they have been arguing on the way to Capernaum, and he intuitively knows about what they have been arguing. So he tells them that whoever wants to be first must be last and servant of all. He then pulls a child into their midst, embraces the child and tells them, "Whoever welcomes one of these little children in my name welcomes me; and whoever welcomes me does not welcome me but the one who sent me." (Mark 9:37) In other words, "You are great when you welcome a child like this, and embrace that child."

Embracing a child

Now I have heard this passage preached on many occasions. Usually the preacher tries to find one endearing characteristic or quality of a child and encourages us to act more like that. Well, children are honest, pure in faith, innocent, and generally non-judgmental. We have learned to romanticize the child from this passage.

However, children are not perfect. Children can be mean, cruel to others, self-centered, rude, and spoiled. Children need to be taught and nurtured. We all need to grow and learn. So why did Jesus choose a child as an example of greatness? What makes a child great? I do not think Jesus was looking for a specific characteristic of a child to highlight. Instead, I think he meant that it was in the embrace of a child that you find greatness. All children have in common a few things due to their age and status. Children are vulnerable and dependent. Thus, they are more disposed to be trusting and have a pure faith because they need to trust and have faith in something greater than themselves.

In the Jewish culture of Jesus' day, children were not highly valued. Not that they were necessarily the focus of abuse, but they definitely were not thought of in high regard. They had not yet reached a mature age, and it was thought that nothing particularly important could come from a child. This is probably why the disciples wanted to keep the children away from Jesus in other scenes. "Well, they are just kids, they are not important...Go away."

In the ancient Jewish culture they instead valued their elders. They had wisdom. They had stood the test of time. The ancient Torah was where wisdom was to be found. The Ten Commandments were about honoring our fathers and mothers. Jews respected their elders. Thus it was thought that children had little to offer and were almost non-persons. It was difficult for many to truly believe, "The wolf will live with the lamb, the leopard will lie down with the goat, the calf and the lion and the yearling together; and a little child will lead them." (Isaiah 11:6)

Our culture today is quite different. It is almost the opposite. We value what is young and new. In fact we probably value it too much. We want things new, sexy and hip. We value young good looks, and almost make people feel bad for getting old.

So, what is Jesus doing here? Is he saying that things in heaven need to be young and hip? Does he want us to be innocent and naive? No, I don't think so. I think Jesus embraces the child as a way to embrace the most vulnerable, fragile, and weakest member in their society. Jesus is embracing the non-person so to speak, the one that desperately needs to trust and have faith in something beyond themselves.[13] Thus, I think he is making a point that greatness is found when we embrace the weakest and most fragile people in our world. Who are the children or not valued or dependent members in our society today?

There is also another point about greatness Jesus is making. When we do embrace such people we also know of our own vulnerability, weakness and fragility. That is when true greatness is found. We often think we need to be strong and in control to be great, but I believe the opposite is true. In fact, I think it is the message of the cross. Jesus is greatest when he allows himself to be fragile and vulnerable on the cross. In this, he fully embraces our brokenness and sin. It is actually true

---

[13] Perkins, "The Gospel of Mark," 637.

strength. We, too, are at our greatest when we know our fragility and vulnerability.

The Greatness of the Inner child

There is an inner, depth psychological sense to this scene of Jesus embracing the child as well. As always Jesus' teachings have an external and internal aspect to them. Internally, Jesus encourages us to find greatness when we get in touch with our inner vulnerability. This vulnerability is often buried in our past, our childhood.

Some in Psychology have talked about the inner child. I particularly enjoyed James Hollis in his book *The Middle Passage* where he wrote about the inner or lost child.[14] Not that we need to become childish again, although that can be rather fun. We are, however, called to get in touch with childlike energy. We are also often called to get in touch with some events that happened when we were children. Events that shape our current lives. We all have things that have happened in life that have hurt us and hindered our development. Many times those can be very painful memories, but becoming aware of them again can lead to tremendous growth, humility, healing, and greatness.

We all know life is difficult for a child. There are intense things that happen in all our lives. As children, this intensity is magnified, and we are often less able to deal with difficult situations. We thus can be scarred, and sometimes doomed to unconsciously repeat over and over again emotional hurt. However, dreams can help us be in touch with those difficult or hurtful memories. By doing so, it may help to free us up to be more who God intends us to be. Not getting in touch with our inner child leaves us acting unconsciously in ways that can be extremely destructive. We can also harbor ill feelings toward those who hurt us. In the end this only hurts us. Not to say what something someone may have done to hurt us is not wrong, it may very well have been, but holding on to hate and hurt affects us the most. But if we can own those experiences, let Jesus hold and embrace our inner child, then we can indeed be closer to our greatness.

---

[14] Hollis, *The Middle Passage: From Misery to Meaning in Midlife*, 103-105.

Inside, Out

There was a great movie recently called *Inside, Out* produced by Jonas Rivera in 2015.[15] The movie is about a little girl's inner development, and her inner emotions. In the movie she had core memories that helped shape who she was. As the movie went on, her insides grew more complex, and she moved from the upper Midwest to San Francisco. She was very upset about this. In order to grow and move past this she had to get in touch with some inner buried emotions in order that they be transformed. This is the perfect movie to illustrate the need to access important core events and feelings that shape our life. In the end the now teenage Riley does move forward in a deeper and more mature way by embracing her inner child in a new way.

My quest to embrace my inner child

In 1994 I became aware again of some painful memories when I was an older child. I discussed in chapter 5 my inner brokenness, which stemmed a lot from incidents of holding in my anger and emotions. One particular incident I described was when I could not emotionally confront my dad and mom. I then went upstairs to my room where I passed out with anger. This was probably the most influential event of my growing-up years. That core memory affected my present and how I dealt with emotions all the time.

In addition, there were other important events in my growing up years. A few of them happened when I was in sixth and seventh grade. I was not a small child, but certainly not grown up. I think the middle school pubescent years can be very influential and damaging to our inner self-esteem. Older children/young teens can be particularly harsh to one another.

During this time I developed a skin issue called vitiligo. It is splotches of non-pigmented skin. I became very ashamed of this condition, and it really affected my self-esteem. I also recall a time when I went to a dance. I got up the nerve to ask a girl I liked to dance. While we were dancing a few of my friends made fun of me. To this day I find it very difficult to dance, and am extremely

---

[15] Ronnie Del Carmen, and Pete Docter. *Inside Out.* DVD. Directed by Pete Docter (Burbank, CA: Walt Disney / Pixar Pictures, 2015).

self-conscious when I do so. It also does not help that I am 6'3"
and 235 lbs. I can never hide on the dance floor. Finally, another
event that really scarred me happened on the basketball court.
Now, basketball was where I let it all hang out. During one game I
yelled at a teammate of mine for not boxing out and rebounding
the basketball. He was just playing very passively. I got very
upset and got in his face. Well, my coach wound up yelling at me
for yelling at the other player. This really affected my game for
years, because I lost my emotional aggressiveness. All of these
were core events in my past that shaped who I was in the present.
They needed to be touched and transformed. I needed Jesus to
hug them.

"Wanting to hide." Thursday 9/8/94.

*I was sitting at the dinner table with Dad, Mom, and
brother. Then my brother started talking and was kidding around.
I don't think I was upset too much, but I got up and left, then I
heard my mom and my brother arguing. My mom was mad at my
brother and started lecturing him; then I just wanted to go away
forever and say forget it.*

Nancy: How did you feel in the dream?
Me: I grew more and more upset as the dream went on.
Nancy: Have you ever been around when your mom and brother
argue?
Me: Oh, yes.
Nancy: What was that like?
Me: I hated it. I would often run outside and go shoot baskets or
something.
Nancy: How did it make you feel?
Me: I just always felt...well I can't describe it.
Nancy: Angry? Scared?
Me: More scared than anything, then it would turn to anger.
Nancy: Have you been around them lately when they have
argued?
Me: I can't remember anything recently.
Nancy: But if they do?
Me: Then I just leave or I want to leave.
Nancy: Do you feel scared again?
Me: More angry...probably a little intimidated.
Nancy: Why do your Mom and brother argue?

Me: In the dream or in real life?
Nancy: Both.
Me: Does it really matter?
Nancy: It can. If the dream shows why they are arguing it could be important, but if they are just arguing then it is the arguing that is the most important thing.
Me: I don't remember why they are arguing in the dream.
Nancy: So the focus is more on how you feel when they argue. It is interesting here that your brother tries to joke with you.
Me: Yeah.
Nancy: Is there a part of you that jokes around when you are in intense situations?
Me: I guess.
Nancy: You guess??
Me: I mean, yes, I do.
Nancy: How do you react now when you are in arguments?
Me: I try to avoid them.
Nancy: So the dream says as well. Do you still get scared?
Me: Sometimes.
Nancy: Sometimes?
Me: Yes...Usually, I guess...or I get mad.
Nancy: Or you run away.
Me: I guess...yes.
Nancy: Is there a healthier way to be in arguments?
Me: Yes. I guess...How do you do that?
Nancy: What?
Me: Change your emotions when you are arguing?
Nancy: Well, if you are aware of what you tend to do, and why you tend to feel that way, then you can more easily make conscious decisions for how to act in that situation.
Me: But you can't stop feeling angry?
Nancy: Or scared.
Me: Or scared?
Nancy: No, but you can begin to control them, and not let them control you.
Me: Is there anything I need to do?
Nancy: No, just pay attention. You are doing well. Let Jesus embrace your inner child.

Reflection questions:
  1. How does one become great? What does greatness mean to you?

2. What childhood memories haunt you? How do they still affect you?
3. What can you do to learn and move forward? How can you embrace your vulnerability and fragility?

Chapter Nine: Mother May I

Near the cross of Jesus stood his mother, his mother's sister, Mary the wife of Clopas, and Mary Magdalene. When Jesus saw his mother there, and the disciple whom he loved standing nearby, he said to her, "Woman, here is your son," and to the disciple, "Here is your mother." From that time on, this disciple took her into his home. (John 19:25b-27, NIV)

Nothing is quite as endearing, nurturing, and important as one's relationship with their mother, and there is no greater example of motherhood than Mary. Mary is chosen to be the mother of Jesus, and she takes on this role with great humility. At the annunciation, Mary receives the proclamation of the angel Gabriel by saying,"I am the Lord's servant. May your word to me be fulfilled." (Luke 1:38) This after initially wondering how this could be so because she is a virgin.

Next, in Luke's gospel, Mary goes to visit her relative Elizabeth who is great with child as well. Her baby is John the Baptist. After John the Baptist leapt in Elizabeth's womb and Elizabeth praises Mary, Mary responds with the Magnificat. "My soul glorifies the Lord and my spirit rejoices in God my Savior..." (Luke 1: 46, 47) Mary's faithful and joyful response to motherhood is a true inspiration for all, not to mention some of the greatest poetry in the entire Bible.

Later, I love how Mary responds to the shepherds' visit and praise at the birth of Jesus, "But Mary treasured up all these things and pondered them in her heart." (Luke 2:19) Mary has a special role indeed, and she is almost an impossible model of motherhood to emulate. However, she does teach us so much about the importance of a human, warm, loving relationship. She is joyful and humble. She knows her child is a gift from God. Her role is to be that of a servant, as all mothers are called to nurture life as servants of God. All mothers and fathers are truly called to be servants. Notice I did not say subordinate, but servant. You can be a servant, model, and disciplinarian at the same time. In fact this seems to me the best way to be a mother and parent.

We often think of Mary as placid and overly gentle. Mary is that nice cute girl in the Christmas pageant right? However, Mary can be stern in her own way. She says to the boy Jesus, after frantically searching for him for three days and finding him in the Temple, "Son, why have you treated us like this?" (Luke 2:48)

One is left to wonder about the entirety of her relationship with Jesus as a boy. Did she discipline him often or very much at all? Did she need to discipline him? We will never know, and perhaps we shouldn't. In any case, Mary was a very caring and nurturing mother. However, it is her relationship with Jesus when he is an adult that intrigues the most.

Mary strongly hints to Jesus to make the wine at the wedding in Cana. "'Woman, why do you involve me?' Jesus replied. 'My hour has not yet come.'" (John 2:4) Mary tells the servants to do as Jesus commands. Jesus then orders the large jars to be filled with water, and when the water is drawn out, it is now fine wine. It is one of the most curious encounters in the Bible. Did Jesus give in to his mother? Was she right? How did they feel toward each other in that moment? The text never really answers these questions and we are left to wonder.

Another curious scene between Mary and Jesus is found in Mark chapter 3. In this chapter many think Jesus is 'out of his mind.' The text says that some of his family went to restrain him. Was his mother part of that group? Did she want to overly protect her son? Later in the chapter Jesus is told that his mother and brothers and sisters are outside looking for him. Jesus responds that his mother and brothers and sisters are those who do the will of God. I am not suggesting that Jesus and Mary had an antagonistic relationship when Jesus was an adult, but you have to wonder how their relationship truly progressed. Did Jesus have to find his own voice apart from his mother? Was that what was going on in Mark chapter 3? One can only speculate, but it is fascinating to ponder.

A new family

I think the most powerful scene between Jesus and his mother, is the one of Jesus on the cross as portrayed in John's gospel. On the cross Jesus looks down and sees the most important people in his earthly life. Two of which are his mother and the 'beloved' disciple. The 'beloved' disciple (often thought to be John) can be symbolic of all beloved disciples of Jesus. It is an incredible literary device used by the writer of John's gospel. It is a way to say to the reader that, "You too can be a 'beloved disciple.'"[16] Jesus says, "'Woman, here is your son,' and to the disciple, 'Here is your mother.'" (John 19:26, 27) Notice, he does not say, "Here you two be friends." No, Jesus is very specific about setting up the mother/son relationship.

In some sense it may be a practical relationship that Jesus initiates. In this male dominated society Mary needs someone to take care of her. However, this is debatable because James, the brother of our Lord, is still very much alive. Even if Mary is not James' biological mother (once again debatable), he would still seem to be the more likely candidate to take care of Mary. No, it seems to me that this new relationship forged at the foot of the cross between mother and new son is a great symbol of a new family. This, I think, is the profound teaching of this scene. Jesus wants his new family of faithful believers, symbolized between his mother and beloved disciple, to be a family of care and nurturing.[17]

There is also another level to this story. This scene is a model that we all need to find mature relationships with our mothers marked by mutuality, care, and concern. Thus, Mary is a tremendous model of a mother from start to finish. She gives birth, nurtures, struggles with, and ultimately has mature relationship with her son.

The mother within

As with all inner figures there is a positive and negative aspect to mothers. The mother can be a very powerful and positive force, what I will call mother earth. The mother can also be a very negative force in our lives, which is often called a mother complex.[18] Both mother earth and mother complex are informed by one's external mother, although they are not identical to our external moms. As always the external informs the inner and the inner influences the external.

---

[16] O'Day, "The Gospel of John," 500.
[17] O'Day, "The Gospel of John," 832.
[18] Coleman, *Dictionary of Psychology*, 150, 464.

Let's first look at the positive inner influence, mother earth. Mother earth is life-giving, nurturing, and protective. Just as the earth is the source of all life, this inner mother earth can be a source of inner nourishment to help us grow. Of course, externally, a mother physically possesses the ability to first birth, and then to nurse an infant to grow. Later as this biological need is weaned, the mother still holds a great deal of importance in the growth process. The powerful bond and relationship between mother and child can never be underestimated.

Sadly, some people do not have the gift of a positive external relationship with their biological mother. While some in this situation develop this important relationship with other feminine figures, tragically some never have a positive relationship with their external mother or a mother figure. This can cause tremendous struggles in developing a life-giving relationship with an inner mother earth, although it is not impossible.

Fortunately, many do have a positive external relationship with their mom, and thus have a great inner mother earth giving tremendous growth and strength. Contrary to what many teenage boys say, there is no shame in having a wonderful relationship with your mother. One can be a momma's boy in a healthy way. In fact, the closer and healthier the external relationship is the better. As a result, in dreams, the inner mother earth can be a very positive figure helping us to be nurtured more and more as life goes on.

When the inner mother is a hindrance to development it is called the mother complex. Everyone has a mother complex, no matter how healthy the relationship with your external mom is. There is always an aspect of a mom that wants to overprotect, emotionally dominate, and hang on to their children. Thus, a mother complex occurs when the inner mother figure dominates and controls relationship, thus hindering and even stunting growth. All of us have to outgrow both parents' influence and find our own identity. This is especially true of a relationship with your parent who is your opposite sex. Once again externally and internally: Sons particularly need to break free of their mothers and daughters from their fathers.

As time goes by the mother complex actually can develop a life of its own. Each person may nurture that complex (unconsciously) to varying degrees, and each person is different. Two different children of the same mother may develop different mother complexes. Even though they have the same mother, they experience her differently. Our own personalities play a factor as well. The mother complex is not all due to the external mother, although influenced by it. The intensity of an inward complex often depends on a person's other characteristics. A strong willed child may not be as affected by an overbearing mother, while a timid child and domineering mother can be a dangerous combination. I do not want to get too much into the argument about genetics versus environment, but it seems to me that basic personality determines much, and experience can help shape our basic personality. Experience and personality inform and influence one another. It is impossible to say which is more important or came first, the chicken or the egg.

In addition, I think there is a generational aspect to all of this. The degree to which this mother complex is a problem often depends on how the parents dealt with and overcame their own mother complexes. As with all things internal, we often pass on the things of which we are unconscious to future generations.

My mother

I am very lucky to have a wonderful mother. My mom was very nurturing, caring, and loving. She was definitely the most important relationship in my early life. My mom is always caring, and has a deep faith. In fact, for me, my mom is important in another way. She was also the one who initially brought me to church and showed me the love of God. Ever since I was a little boy I was brought to church. My mom was very active in church. She helped teach Sunday School, helped lead Vacation Bible School, and helped out in many other ways in the church. There are many memories embedded in my psyche because my mom brought me to church. Not only that, but she has a great faith that has always been a model to me. As I grew up, I could talk to her about church and God. The impact of this is tremendous.

My mom taught me many other things as well. She deeply instilled in me the need to be truthful. She said to me, "Dan, I can take anything but you lying to me." To this day I find it extremely difficult to lie. My mother also taught me to have great sympathy and develop great empathy for others. She would often ask, "How do you think that made that person feel?" She always preached about how our actions affect others. Once again this is a gift that still serves me well today as I often try to look at things from others' perspectives.

However, like all moms, my mom had her shortcomings. Early in life I could be very intimidated by my mother. I remember often wondering and worrying about how she felt. She would drive with big sunglasses and I would wonder if there was anger in her eyes. When my brothers or I did something wrong, then she would glare at us. Many moms develop 'the look,' and my mom definitely had it. I can still see that look if I close my eyes and think about it. My mom could also overly worry about what others thought of how she did things. This insecurity could affect how I related to my mom. I would generally want to please her. As the years went by this faded, but it remained emotionally powerful and influential internally. This desire to please my mom externally had a great influence on the development of an overactive mother complex.

My inner mother influences my journey

In 1994 from an internal perspective, my mom was still very active. My mom was in many dreams, and it was very evident that my inner mother had a great deal of influence. This was especially true due to the fact I was in my mid-twenties. This inner mother could be mother earth or mother complex. Initially in my dreams she appeared as mother complex that had to become conscious. Like all young men I needed to become my own man, and even though my mom was mostly a very positive figure in my life, internally my mother complex could be emotionally overwhelming.

All this led to interesting internal and external dynamics. My external mom had a great faith and a deep intellect. She, too, did much inner work in her late forties and fifties, which is why she was the one who was able to reach out to me in my darkest time and suggest connecting with Nancy. My external mom helped me in many ways while my inner mother complex hindered me in other ways. There is a profound learning in all of this. Every external and internal relationship we have has seeds for growth. It is amazing how God's grace works through people in our outer life and within our psyche.

"The Vicious Cats." Thursday 10/6/94.

I was with my family, at least my mother and father, and it started outside. This guy came and somehow we had won a prize. He was going to give it to us the next morning. It was some group of animals. Well, I went to go to sleep and these animals must have gotten loose. They were like little vicious cats. They started out ok, but once you aggravated them they started attacking me and gnawing at me. I ran into my parents room where only my mom was. They didn't seem to attack her and she really didn't help me. The guy was staying in my brother's room, and he came and got them off of me. I woke up with some serious scars. I killed a lot of the cats with my bare hands, but some lived.

Nancy - How did you feel in the dream?
Me - I was annoyed and scared. I couldn't get away from those damn cats.
Nancy - Do you not like cats?
Me - I actually love cats, but these were not nice cats.
Nancy - How would you describe cats?
Me - They can be very independent, strong willed, but loveable.
Nancy - When are cats vicious?
Me - When they want something they can't have.
Nancy - Would you say cats are masculine or feminine?
Me - I would say feminine.
Nancy - Why?
Me - I am not sure. Maybe because they can be very cute and loveable, and then switch to being extremely intense.
Nancy - So cats have a range of emotions. Are women that way?
Me - They are much better with their emotions than most men I know.
Nancy - And so this man wants to give you a prize but it turns vicious on you.
Me - Right.
Nancy - In the dream you go to your parents' room. Why do you think you did that?
Me - I guess I wanted safety.
Nancy -Did your parents keep you safe growing up?
Me - Yeah for the most part.
Nancy - It's interesting here, your mom is there but your dad is not. Did you go to your mom more for help?
Me - Yes. I did. I was probably closer to my mom.

Nancy - But here she won't help you. You have to face these vicious cats on your own. It is also interesting that the cats don't attack her. They seem to be in cahoots.

Me - Yeah.

Nancy - Do you think there are ways you still seek your mother's protection?

Me - I don't think so. I'm pretty independent.

Nancy - Are you emotionally independent?

Me - I don't know.

Nancy - You don't know? Well, the dream is saying that a prize you were given turns vicious and attacks you. You look for help by seeking your parents, particularly your mom, but she won't help you. You then kill some of these cats, but are scarred by others.

Me - So what should I do?

Nancy - Have you ever heard of a mother complex?

Me - Yes.

Nancy - Well, why don't you sit and pray about the ways you could still be attached to your mother, internally, emotionally?

Me - Like how?

Nancy - Is there an inner emotional part of you that feels feminine that dominates and attacks you?

Me - Like unable to feel?

Nancy - No more like stunted.

Me - Stunted?

Nancy - Yes. Like how do you feel underdeveloped emotionally, and what keeps you from developing in that way?

Me - Alright, I will try.

Nancy - You will try or you will do?

Me - I will do.

"Dancing with my Mom." Monday 10/30/94.

I was walking around leading my mom through a maze. The maze was made up of funny things and jokes like the movie Airplane. I told my mom to pay attention and it would be really funny. Then we ended up in a big ballroom where people were dancing, and I started dancing with my mom.

Nancy - How did you feel in the dream?

Me - Kind of weird, but happy.

Nancy - It's another dream with your mom.

Me - Right.

Nancy - But this time you are leading her around. What do you think of when you think of a maze?

Me - I think of the Greeks. Of being lost.

Nancy - It's hard to find your way through a maze.

Me - Yeah, but it can be fun.

Nancy - Are you adventurous?

Me - I can be.

Nancy - And here you see all these scenes from the movie *Airplane*?

Me - Yeah.

Nancy - Did you like the movie *Airplane*.

Me - Yeah I thought it was funny. What I would call stupid silly.

Nancy - Does your mom have a sense of humor?

Me - Yes. I remember watching George Carlin with her.

Nancy - So you are leading your mom through this silly maze. It's as if you want to tell her something or show her something.

Me - Maybe I want her to know I can lead the way.

Nancy. Huh. Interesting. Then you end up dancing with her. Have you ever danced with your mom?

Me - I don't know. I can't remember.

Nancy - What does it mean to dance with someone?

Me - I don't know. I am not a good dancer.

Nancy - You've never danced?

Me - Yes, I've danced...just not real well.

Nancy - Well, what was it like?

Me - It is kind of like you are exploring how the other person moves. You have to learn to move together, but also respect each other's movements.

Nancy - So how would you do that with your Mom?

Me - I guess I would show her how I can lead, and how I could have new moves.

Nancy - So you are kind of learning a new relationship with your mom.

Me - Yes, I guess.

Nancy - You go from lost in a maze with silly scenes to dancing. Maybe a shift in the relationship.

Me - My external or internal mother?

Nancy - Both. Keep dancing.

Reflection questions:
1. Describe your mother? How did you relate to her growing up?

81

2. How do you think your mother affects you now, externally and internally?
3. How have you grown emotionally mature and independent?

Chapter Ten: A Sleeping Giant

*Some time later God tested Abraham. He said to him,
"Abraham!" "Here I am," he replied. Then God said, "Take your
son, your only son, whom you love—Isaac—and go to the region
of Moriah. Sacrifice him there as a burnt offering on a mountain I
will show you." Early the next morning Abraham got up and
loaded his donkey. He took with him two of his servants and his
son Isaac. When he had cut enough wood for the burnt offering,
he set out for the place God had told him about. On the third day
Abraham looked up and saw the place in the distance. He said to
his servants, "Stay here with the donkey while I and the boy go
over there. We will worship and then we will come back to you."
Abraham took the wood for the burnt offering and placed it on his
son Isaac, and he himself carried the fire and the knife. As the two
of them went on together, Isaac spoke up and said to his father
Abraham, "Father?" "Yes, my son?" Abraham replied. "The fire
and wood are here," Isaac said, "but where is the lamb for the
burnt offering? Abraham answered, "God himself will provide the
lamb for the burnt offering, my son." And the two of them went on
together. When they reached the place God had told him about,
Abraham built an altar there and arranged the wood on it. He
bound his son Isaac and laid him on the altar, on top of the
wood. Then he reached out his hand and took the knife to slay his
son. But the angel of the Lord called out to him from heaven,
"Abraham! Abraham!" "Here I am," he replied. "Do not lay a hand
on the boy," he said. "Do not do anything to him. Now I know that
you fear God, because you have not withheld from me your son,
your only son." (Genesis 22:1-12, NIV)*

As Abraham lifts the knife, all of future Israel holds their
breath. If there is no Isaac there is no Jacob. If there is no Jacob
there are no 12 sons of Jacob. Jacob was renamed Israel by the
river Jabbok. Thus the 12 sons of Jacob are the twelve tribes of
Israel. If Isaac dies, there is no future Israel.

Abraham. The 'present' Father

Who knows what is going through the mind of Abraham as he lifts the knife. Perhaps he is thinking about how God originally called him. "The Lord had said to Abram, 'Go from your country, your people and your father's household to the land I will show you. I will make you into a great nation, and I will bless you; I will make your name great, and you will be a blessing." (Genesis 12:1-2) Or perhaps he is remembering how God once told him, "'Look up at the sky and count the stars—if indeed you can count them.' Then he said to him, 'So shall your offspring be.'" (Genesis 15:5) Maybe he is thinking of how Sarah laughed at the notion of having a child in her advanced years, then having that greatly promised child and naming him Isaac, which means laughter.[19] Perhaps Abraham cannot think of anything, but the pain.

This is not the story of blind faith. No, it is the ultimate story of presence. Abraham is present to God. God calls to Abraham by name. Abraham says, "Here I am." Abraham is also present to his son. Isaac addresses Abraham as "father." Abraham says, "Yes, my son." As he lifts the knife, fully present in faith with eyes wide open, the angel calls out his name, "Abraham, Abraham." Abraham once again says, "Here I am."

I chose Abraham as my quintessential father figure not just because his name means "father of a multitude." Of course he is known most of his life as Abram which means "exalted father."[20] No, I chose Abraham because he epitomizes faithful presence as a father. He is present to God throughout his life. He is present to his sons. He does what is necessary, and is generally not selfish. He is present to everyone else. That I think is the great trait of a father. Mothers are called to be present as well, but they tend to be that naturally. Dads are the ones who seem to have more of a choice to be present or not to be present. Further, like mothers, fathers are best when they are servants. Servants who are present pointing to God.

Our heavenly Father

---

[19] Cornwall and Smith ed., *The Exhaustive Dictionary of Bible Names*, 84.
[20] Cornwall and Smith ed., *The Exhaustive Dictionary of Bible Names*, 4.

I want to take a moment to discuss the pluses and minuses of identifying God as father. Many people talk about how their experience with their human father relates to their understanding of God. I think this may be true to a degree, but that is mostly because we have identified God often only as Father. Unfortunately, we often do not acknowledge God's feminine side. As a result, we limit God to the Father role. I for one do not think of God as an old man with a white-beard sitting on some cloud. Although I do still observe tradition and refer to God often as Father, Son, and Holy Spirit. The Trinity is as good a way as one can to describe the different aspects of God (as has been revealed to us). More importantly, it highlights the relational love of God. Jesus called out to his "Abba," a dear and intimate term for a father.[21] I think Jesus was doing this to highlight the intimacy of his relationship more than highlighting God as male. In truth, the minute we try to think about and describe God we are limiting the limitless. However, we have to talk about God, so we must use limiting labels and concepts that point to the reality of God. Thus, if you have to use an image for God, then a loving Father helps start the conversation well for many. However, we should be cautious to only understand God as father, and we should never only let our experience with our earthly fathers shape our understanding of God.

Healthy Father figures

Fathers, like mothers, are very important for our development externally and internally. A good healthy father figure provides great guidance and wisdom in life. A father often shows a child how to do certain things in the world. Fathers can be powerful mentor figures, and this mentor role can continue into adulthood even when we need to do our own self defining.

I love the Superman movies, especially the most recent *Man of Steel* directed by Zack Snyder and released in 2013.[22] Superman has two exceptional father figures. His biological Father, Jor El,

---

[21] Green and Robinson ed., *A Concise Lexicon to the Biblical Languages*, Greek 1.
[22] David S. Goyer, and Christopher Nolan. *Man of Steel*. DVD. Directed by Zack Snyder (Burbank, CA: Warner Bros. Pictures, 2013).

who is a source of great wisdom throughout Superman's life. He is wise, calm, and full of knowledge. I love how Superman can access Jor EL from a special kind of memory bank. It is one of the cool things in the Superman movies. In some sense our experiences with our fathers provide a great memory bank of wisdom for us. Superman is also lucky to have a father figure here on earth. After Superman crashes to earth, a human couple takes him in and become his mother and father. This earthly father figure also helps Superman find his way in life by offering wise practical counsel. Further, he shows Superman a passion for doing the right things, being just, fair, and helping others. A good father can make all the difference.

Come on Dad

A father figure can be negative in two ways. First a father can be overprotective and domineering. There are countless movies and stories of people who are hopelessly stuck in their father's shadow. I presume that this is a difficult thing. Daughters may have a particularly rough time in the shadow of their father, just as sons can struggle under the weight of their mother's domineering influence. Some people in these situations resort to lashing out in unhealthy ways. Others wind up always trying to measure everything and everyone against their "daddy." This can be done either consciously or unconsciously.

A second way a father figure can be destructive is by being absent. This is the Father who skips town, either physically or emotionally or both. People who grow up with an absent father really struggle to find themselves. They often have not been given enough positive reinforcement, wisdom, guidance, and teaching to find their true gifts and apply them in life. Sons sometimes particularly need a father figure to help free them from an overactive mother relationship. Everyone needs a present father, not an absent one.

The absentee father figure is sadly all too common. Many grow up without a father in their home. However, some luckily find a father figure besides their biological dad. Coaches, teachers, and pastors can be great models that help (even with someone who has a present father). Though some are never blessed to have any positive father figure. The result of an absent father can lead to despair, abuse, and addictions. The absent father is one of the great curses of our age.

Wake up Dad

From an internal perspective an absent father is a sleeping giant. One that can be awakened, even if reconciliation with a biological father is not possible or doesn't happen. Absent fathers can lurk in our dreams hinting at a way forward. Deep down we desperately want to connect with a healthy father figure so we too can become superman or superwoman. Like the relationship with a mother, the more authentic, honest, loving, and present, the better.

In 1994, my inner father figure was absent. He was a sleeping giant. This was made very clear to me early on in dream analysis. In a dream shared earlier in this book, my father brought me to a doctor's office, but he was the one who was sick. In other dreams my father would be absent, or silent. He needed to be awakened.

My real father is a great guy. He is extremely hard working. He was a director of quality assurance for a company, and he would work long hours. This led to his often being absent. He was also a stern disciplinarian when I grew up. However, if you got him in the right mood, he was a fun jokester. If I did something to hurt myself accidentally my dad would say with a straight face, as I suffered some shameful little pain, "Daniel, could you do that again, I didn't see what you did the first time?"

My earliest childhood memories of my father were powerful. To this day I can still picture the hat he wore when I was a small child. It was a bluish/grey fedora that many white-collar working men in the sixties and early seventies wore. I remember him coming home from work. It would be such a joy when he had time to toss the baseball with me.

One of the most powerful memories of my dad always brings tears to my eyes. My dad was washing the car in the driveway. My brothers and I were playing in the yard. At some point I decided to get in the driver's seat of the car. Unbeknownst to my dad, I somehow put the car in neutral and the car started to roll down the driveway into the street. In the flash of an eye my dad ran and pulled me out of the car. The car had begun to roll too fast for him to jump in and try to stop it. He lovingly saved me from certain injury. My dad protected me. I will always have that image of my dad, lovingly saving me

When I was in middle school, my dad went through something in his life. To this day I am not sure I know all that took place, but he became very absent emotionally. My dad was never one for being good with emotions. His mother was pretty overbearing and he was an only child. During my early teens dad seemed to have a particular rough time emotionally. He would work way too late. He seemed very distant and always angry. He would hardly ever come to my sports games. On Sundays he would work in the yard, while I went to church. I wound up finding other spiritual father figures like Reverend Rick and Reverend John.

At one point in time during middle school, my dad really embarrassed and upset me. My dad was an engineer. He wanted his boys to be good at math, and I was naturally good at math. When it came time to take a test to qualify for eighth grade algebra, I missed it by a few points. My dad went through the roof. How could I have possibly messed this up? My dad stormed into the school to talk to my teacher when he found out. I was so embarrassed by his actions. I felt about an inch high. "You can't make it to my games, but you can embarrass me like this," I thought to myself. His overreaction made quite a lasting imprint in me. I felt very distant from my dad for a time.

As time went on my dad seemed to lighten up. I started to make some greater connection with him later in high school and when I was in college. One of my favorite memories is when my fraternity had a Dad's Day outing. It was a blast. We rented some casino games and each father/son got a certain amount of Monopoly money to gamble with. Out of about 100 father/son combos, we were the first to lose all of our money. It happened pretty quickly actually. I had a special laugh with my dad. The beverages were not bad either.

Dad never understood my connection and passion at church, but he didn't discourage it either. In many ways I grew emotionally at church, but still had an emotional gap in my psyche from when my father was emotionally absent. Nancy would make me keenly aware of this, and help guide me to awaken my inner father, which also positively affected my relationship with my external dad. Dream analysis helped all my external relationships, and for that I am eternally grateful.

"In the Army" Thursday 11/3/94.

I dreamed I joined the Army. All these other guys had big tasks and everything. I got a green ticket to Ogden Utah, where I would do maintenance work on cars. I was very happy about this. When we were dispatched I walked up to a door that led to my parents' room. Neither of them were there. Then I went into my room and began to pack. I remember thinking my father would be proud.

Nancy - How did you feel in the dream?
Me - I felt sad, then lost, and then hopeful.
Nancy - Why did you feel sad?
Me - In the beginning I was sad because everybody had great tasks but me.
Nancy - Do you sometimes feel that way?
Me - In real life?
Nancy - Yes.
Me - I guess, sometimes. I often feel lost, like I can't decide what to do in life. Everyone else I know seems to have a plan.
Nancy - Then you said you felt lost?
Me - Yeah. I felt lost when I went to my parents' room and found no one.
Nancy - Have your parents ever been absent in your life?
Me - No, not really. They have always been very supportive.
Nancy - Both your mom and your dad?
Me - Well, my mom was generally always supportive and present...
Nancy - But your Dad?
Me - My Dad always cared, especially about school, but he rarely supported me at my sports games.
Nancy - Why do you think that is?
Me - Dad would bury himself at work.
Nancy - And miss your games.
Me - Yeah.
Nancy - Did it bother you?
Me - I guess it did. I got used to it.
Nancy - In the dream you join the Army. Did you ever want to join the Army?
Me - No. I never considered it.
Nancy - Why not?
Me - It just wasn't me. I was not big into discipline at the time.

Nancy - Do you know of anyone who served in the Army?
Me - I had a few fraternity brothers in the military..and my dad served as well.
Nancy - When did he serve?
Me - In the early sixties, I think.
Nancy - What did he do?
Me - I think he served in the motor pool. Dad is very mechanical. He has a degree in mechanical engineering.
Nancy - Amazing. And in your dream you get a green ticket to Utah to work on cars. Do you think you would have fun doing that?
Me - Probably not. My dad taught me some things about cars, but I am not a big mechanic.
Nancy - But at the end of the dream you think your parents will feel proud?
Me - Yeah. Do I need to go become a mechanic?
Nancy - No, but I do think you need to find out more about your father.
Me - Like what?
Nancy - Like what did he do when he was your age? How did he find his way? How long did he serve in the military? What decisions did he make when he was your age?
Me - Just talk to him like that?
Nancy - Is that a problem?
Me - No. I guess not.
Nancy - The more you know about your dad, the better, especially at your age. Internally he is sick, he is asleep. You need to wake him up.

"Hail, Hail to old Purdue" Friday 11/11/94.

My dad took me to a Purdue vs Notre Dame football game. We had really bad seats. There was a section that was way up high. We walked up to take our seats. The stadium kept filling up and they were expecting a record crowd. Then the section I was in started to shake. No one seemed worried, but I was a little worried. I can't remember if this happened before or after the game but I was walking and I tripped and my right leg fell into a hole and hurt myself. My dad helped me. Purdue won.

Nancy - So how did you feel in the dream?
Me - Mostly scared.

Nancy - Why do you think you were scared?

Me - I was scared because we sat too high up, and the stands began to shake.

Nancy - So you had bad seats and things felt unstable. Why Purdue vs Notre Dame do you think?

Me - My dad went to Purdue.

Nancy - He did. Did he ever take you to a football game?

Me - Yeah. When we were little we went a few times. Dad loves Purdue.

Nancy - Did he ever take you to a Notre Dame/Purdue game?

Me - I was trying to think of that when I was driving here. I think he did.

Nancy - Would that have any special meaning?

Me - The Notre Dame game is a big game for Purdue.

Nancy - Much like getting to know your father is an important game you could say?

Me - Yeah.

Nancy - Lots of people want to see that.

Me - Yeah. Plus one of the Four Horsemen of Notre Dame is a distant relative of my Grandpa. His name was Elmer Layden.

Nancy - So you are at an important game.

Me - Yeah. That is one thing I often did with dad, watch sports, particularly Purdue sports.

Nancy - But he didn't make it to many of your games.

Me - No, but we watched sports together.

Nancy - In the dream you get hurt.

Me - Yeah. I fell into a hole.

Nancy - You hurt your leg?

Me - Yeah.

Nancy - That would make it hard to get around. Have you ever hurt your leg?

Me - I have twisted my ankle a million times playing basketball.

Nancy - It hurts?

Me - Yeah it does.

Nancy - Did your dad ever help you when you were hurt?

Me - No. That would be my mom. My dad would say some smart-ass thing like, "Daniel, could you do that again? I didn't see it the first time."

Nancy - That's funny.

Me - Although he did rescue me once.

Nancy - Really?

Me - Yeah. When I was real little. He was washing the car. Somehow I got in the driver's seat and put the car in neutral. The car started to roll down the driveway. My dad raced and saved me.

Nancy - Your dad saved you. That is a powerful image to hold on to.

Me - Yeah.

Nancy - I think your sleeping giant is waking up and starting to help you.

Reflection questions:
1. Describe your Father. How did you relate to your Father growing up?
2. How does your relationship with your Father affect you now?
3. What are ways you need to grow beyond and independent from your Father, externally or internally?

Chapter Eleven: Dancing with your Anima

So the man gave names to all the livestock, the birds in the sky and all the wild animals. But for Adam no suitable helper was found. So the Lord God caused the man to fall into a deep sleep; and while he was sleeping, he took one of the man's ribs and then closed up the place with flesh. Then the Lord God made a woman from the rib he had taken out of the man, and he brought her to the man. The man said, "This is now bone of my bones and flesh of my flesh; she shall be called 'woman,' for she was taken out of man." That is why a man leaves his father and mother and is united to his wife, and they become one flesh. (Genesis 2:20-24, NIV)

Relationships are vitally important for human beings. We learn who we are through relationships. We are who we are in relationship, and one of the most important relationships we can have is with a spouse.

In the Genesis account, Eve is made by taking a rib out of Adam. However, this in no way signifies that men are superior to women. No, instead Genesis is teaching a truth that men and women are eternally connected. Adam rejoices, "This is now bone of my bones and flesh of my flesh..." (Genesis 2:23) This person Eve is not just anybody. She is part of him, and he is part of her.

Next the text says those most famous words, "That is why a man leaves his father and mother and is united to his wife, and they become one flesh." (Genesis 2:24) Jesus quotes this when asked about divorce. He even adds that, "Therefore what God has joined together, let no one separate." (Matthew 19:6) Once again underscoring that this is no ordinary relationship.

Marriage as a vocation

Marriage is definitely a vocation, meaning it is a calling. People are called into this type of relationship. It is a gift and a responsibility. By the way, not everyone is called into the married life. Some people are truly called to a single life, and singles are not the less for it. One can develop spiritually as a single and still have many vitally important relationships. One thing this teaching from Genesis points out is that one needs to leave their father and mother and be joined to their spouse. This is often thought of as an external process. That is, one needs to move out of their parents' garage, get married, and get a real job. This is an exciting time for people (often most notably the parents). However, it can be difficult. In pre-marriage counseling I spend a great deal of time talking about how the couple is going to live from this point forward. They will be joining together and there is much to this. They need to learn how to live together. They need to learn where the toothbrushes go and important stuff like that. They also need to learn how to communicate, and to live sacrificially.

I also spend a great deal of time talking about their personalities and family origins. Generally, people learn a lot about marriage from their parents. Parents model marriage in good and bad ways. Some people can have other models of marriage from their grandparents or another important couple in their life. Unfortunately, people tend to expect their new spouse to be exactly like what they have seen modeled. We all know someone who wants to marry someone just like their dad or mom. Often this desire is unconscious, even if everyone around them can see it. Each of us, however, is called to move beyond the models we have been given. We are called to forge a new relationship with our new spouse. Being aware of your expectations is vital for a successful marriage.

Being Given away

In the wedding rite there is a place for the "Giving in marriage." It is an important and powerful part of any wedding ceremony. Traditionally, it was when the father of the bride passed on his daughter to the new husband's care and responsibility. Hopefully, we are past this outdated, misguided male-domineering practice. However, the "Giving in marriage" can still be vitally important, and a symbol of the Biblical truth that one must leave your mother and father and be joined to your spouse. Nowadays, the liturgical practice can reflect that both partners are moving into a new, committed, adult relationship. Instead of just having the priest say, "Who gives this woman to this man?" and the father of the bride saying, "I do," the priest can say, "Who presents these two persons to be married to each other?" and both sets of parents stand up and say, "We do."[23]

Like all good liturgy, what we do is an outward sign of an inward and spiritual grace.[24] "The Giving away" reinforces to the parents that something new beyond their control and responsibility will happen. It also reinforces to the couple that they are no longer under the protection of their parents. They are adults starting a new family unit and called to witness to the world the love God has given them. This is the external process of leaving your father and mother and being joined to your spouse.

A Marriage Within

The outward need to leave parents and be joined to their spouse is also an inward journey. As noted in chapters 9 and 10, it is important for a person to inwardly move beyond the protection and dominance of their parents. Each of us has external parents who are unique. Each of us is called to move those relationships to adult loving, healthy, respectful relationships. As also discussed we have unique internal parents, informed and influenced by our external parents. We are called to bring those inner relationships to mature, healthy, and loving relationship within ourselves as well. The less we do this inner work, the more likely it is that these internal parents will hinder our ability to connect well with an external or internal spouse.

In dream analysis, Jung talked about the inner feminine anima for a male, and an inner masculine animus for a female.[25] It is vitally important for us to connect with these figures internally. There is much to say here, so I will try to highlight as much as I can about this important inner work. First, like everything else, the external informs the internal and the internal

---

[23] *The Book of Common Prayer*, 437.
[24] *The Book of Common Prayer*, 858.
[25] Jung and Storr, *The Essential Jung: Selected Writings*, 112.

influences the external. Thus, like an external spouse, the internal anima is a source of creating. When we are able to connect with this internal anima it breathes new life into us. It also affects other people in our external lives. Relating to the inner anima impacts our journey to become our true self. Second, the anima figure may be represented by many different (in a man's case) females in your dreams. There can be one feminine figure that dominates in your dreams because the qualities she possesses are very important to you, but even then the unconscious can use various females to highlight different qualities of the inner anima. Connecting with more than one female figure internally is not cheating on anybody. It is merely bringing more fullness to the inner. Interestingly, the unconscious does often use your external spouse or an important female of your age. You are often attracted to that person externally for a reason. It is because they are attractive to you internally as well.

Many times we can become attracted to someone externally because our unconscious is trying to teach us an important internal aspect of ourselves that person represents. Many who are unaware can be led away from their current external spouse by another external prospective mate, when the wisest thing is not to abandon our current spouse, but to incorporate internally what qualities the other prospective mate may possess. By doing this, you may enhance your relationship with your current spouse instead of unwisely leaving a spouse you are committed to.

I also want to touch on the subject of sex in dreams. Sex is the most intimate, vulnerable, loving act we can physically do with another person. Thus, when we have a dream about sex, it represents our inward desire to lovingly, intimately connect with that part of ourselves the person represents. We may or may not also want to be in a sexual relationship with that person in our external lives. Sometimes we can have a dream about having sex with another person that we really do not want to engage in sex. This is the unconscious telling us we are intimately connected inside ourselves to something we do not like which is represented by that person. That can be a good lesson, or a hard one. We may be called to deepen this aspect the person represents, or we may be made aware of something unhealthy. Finally, we may have sex in a dream with someone we really want to externally. It is best to know what this means internally for you, rather than just acting it out in your external life, no matter how tempting it may be. You may also be called by

God to have an external sexual relationship with that person, or you may not. All external and internal relationships take discernment, especially intimate ones. Cherish them. They are all gifts.

You are too "Shy, Shy"

In 1994 I was in the process of leaving my father and mother to be joined to my wife, spiritually speaking. I was not dating anyone at the time, but my insides were churning. In fact, I think much of my anxiety was unconscious inner anxiety about this process. It was probably no coincidence that this intense spiritual desert experience began around my last year of college as I was moving into the real world.

It was also no coincidence that my deep inner anxieties began around the time when I started to pursue a romantic relationship my last year of college. I was always very shy around women. I had had many crushes growing up, but I never really got close to anyone. One could say that I was unconsciously frozen. Thus, when I went to pursue close relationship, and was moving into the real world externally, I was actually starting the process of leaving my father and mother and being joined to something new.

I was head over heels in love with this girl in college. She could do no wrong in my eyes. She was sweet, kind, beautiful, and had a great Christian heart. I had shyly swooned over her and been her friend for years. I finally got up the courage to tell her how I felt. Sadly, I entered my intense desert time shortly afterward. I was unable to be fully available in the relationship because of the storm inside me. We broke it off after trying a few times. I can't say I blame her. I was just unavailable emotionally.

Nancy taught me that for healthy external intimate relationships, I need to be conscious of what was going on inside me. Further, connecting to my inner anima would be a great source of spiritual, creative energy that would birth many things in my life. In a way it would be the source of all healthy relationships. It would also be a source of energy in my budding professional vocation. The more we are connected to our inner anima the more we are able to have that inner creativity spill out into all we do. This emotionally immature, shy, unconscious guy was being thrust by God through this desert experience to come to know amazing inward graces. Once we begin to connect inwardly to this energy, as Jesus says, "Therefore what God has joined together, let no one separate." (Matthew 19:6)

"My mom and my anima." Thursday 10/27/94

I ran into Jill at a play and we really did not say too much. I kept wanting to get closer, but she was not sure, but she kept letting me closer. I was kind of shy. Then she left to go to some room and I followed her. When I entered the room my mom and Jill were both there. They were both lying down. My mom looked very comfortable while Jill seemed very uncomfortable. Jill did not want me in the room.

Nancy - How did you feel in the dream?
Me - I was confused.
Nancy - Why do you think you felt confused?
Me - Well, I wanted to get close to Jill, but I was not sure.
Nancy - Not sure of what?
Me - How she felt.
Nancy - Jill seems pretty important to you. She is in a lot of your dreams.
Me - Yeah, we were good friends. We worked together as co-leaders of a youth group. We also dated off and on our senior year.
Nancy - So she is very important to you. Were you attracted to her?
Me - Yes.
Nancy - And you did a lot of spiritual things together. Can you describe her?
Me - Well, she is very beautiful. She is very kind, and likes to have fun. She is a very strong Christian. I just like being with her.
Nancy - But in the dream you are confused?
Me - Right.
Nancy - Did you often wonder about her feelings in your outer life?
Me - Yeah. I never knew how she felt about me.
Nancy - Did she know how you felt about her?
Me - Eventually.
Nancy - Eventually?
Me - Yeah, after a few years I finally told her how I felt.
Nancy - A few years? Why do you think it took you so long?
Me - I am a little shy with my feelings.
Nancy - I'll say. Are you still in touch with her?

Me - Not really. She kind of moved on.

Nancy - So why do you think she is in your dreams so often?

Me - I don't know. I guess she is trying to tell me something.

Nancy - Yeah, I'll say. Do you know what an anima is?

Me - It is like an inner feminine figure, right?

Nancy - Yes. Jung talked a lot about it. The inner feminine or anima for a male, and the inner masculine or animus for a female. It represents an important creative force in you. I suggest you read up a little about it.

Me - So is Jill my inner anima?

Nancy - She represents a piece of it. She is very important too because she has been an important spiritual companion for you as well.

Me - OK.

Nancy - So what is your Mom doing here in the dream?

Me - It seems like she is getting in the way.

Nancy - Do you think you are still more connected emotionally to your mom?

Me - I hope not.

Nancy - The dream kind of says you are, at least internally.

Me - How do I change that?

Nancy - Keep paying attention. It'll change. Do you like to do anything creative?

Me - Not really. I am a little more of a sports freak.

Nancy - Yes, that is obvious. You might want to try some new things, creative things.

Me - Like what?

Nancy - Start with what you know, and be creative.

"Struggle with a feminine within." Friday 10/28/94

Jill and I upset at a college Christian fellowship event. It started out that I was at a rehearsal for a college Christian fellowship event. And they wanted me to take part and lead with one of the microphones. Some girl talked me into it, and when it was happening she sat right next to me. During the event Jill came in and walked right in front of me. She was wearing a white sweater and green pants. It didn't seem like the perfect outfit for her. She didn't seem to see me and I didn't say anything. Then she kind of sat down behind me (not directly). Then she started to talk to me, "Dan, is that you? What are you doing here? You didn't tell me you'd be here." And I didn't turn around right away, I kind of ignored her. And then I did turn around and she seemed kind of upset. So I apologized to her and explained that I did not know ahead of time that I would be there.

Nancy - How did you feel in the dream?
Me - I felt upset.
Nancy - Why were you upset.
Me - Because Jill was upset with me.
Nancy - Another dream with Jill. She really is important to you.
Me - Yeah.
Nancy - Here you go to a college Christian fellowship event.
Me - Yeah.
Nancy - What is that?
Me - It is a Christian college campus ministry.
Nancy - Did you go to those events?
Me - Only once. Jill went all the time. She is very active in it.
Nancy - Did you like it?
Me - I always felt uncomfortable there.
Nancy - Because?
Me - They seemed so sure of themselves, and I was not confident in my faith at the time.
Nancy - Were you jealous?
Me - Yeah, I guess.
Nancy - In the dream some girl, not Jill, talks you into leading.
Me - Yes.
Nancy - What do you think that means?
Me - I don't know.
Nancy - Do you like to lead things.
Me - Yeah, generally.
Nancy - So something in you is encouraging you to lead at some place you are not comfortable. Do you think this is a good thing?
Me - I hope so.
Nancy - Are you learning anything new right now?
Me - Yeah. I guess I am learning a lot about leading church events in my job as a youth leader.
Nancy - Do you like that?
Me - Yeah. I like learning more about church life and work.
Nancy - In the dream you try to ignore Jill. Why do you think that is?
Me - In the dream I wanted to make her jealous.
Nancy - Do you think that is a mature thing to do?
Me - No.

Nancy - But you do it anyway? Then she gets upset with you.
Me - I guess that is not good.
Nancy - At least you are engaging each other. That is an improvement. Starting to dance with your anima.
Me - You're talking internally.
Nancy - Yes. Of course.
Me - Is the internal more important?
Nancy - Both our external and internal relationships are important. What did Jesus say? "First clean the inside of the cup and dish, and then the outside also will be clean." (Matthew 23:26)
Me - So this is not all about my external relationship with Jill?
Nancy - Oh, no. This is all about your inner life. It may improve your external relationships, but your dreams are all about you.
Me - So my inner relationship with my anima as represented by Jill is still struggling.
Nancy - Yes, but it is moving.
Me - Why is it moving?
Nancy - Because you are paying attention. Keep dancing.

Reflection questions:
1. Who are your important relationships in life? Who is attractive to you?
2. Do you dream about those people? How do you think they affect your inner life?
3. How can you better improve your creativity and the health of your important relationships?

Chapter Twelve: Keep the mirror in your face

But the thing David had done displeased the Lord. The Lord sent Nathan to David. When he came to him, he said, "There were two men in a certain town, one rich and the other poor. The rich man had a very large number of sheep and cattle, but the poor man had nothing except one little ewe lamb he had bought. He raised it, and it grew up with him and his children. It shared his food, drank from his cup and even slept in his arms. It was like a daughter to him. "Now a traveler came to the rich man, but the rich man refrained from taking one of his own sheep or cattle to prepare a meal for the traveler who had come to him. Instead, he took the ewe lamb that belonged to the poor man and prepared it for the one who had come to him." David burned with anger against the man and said to Nathan, "As surely as the Lord lives, the man who did this must die! He must pay for that lamb four times over, because he did such a thing and had no pity." Then Nathan said to David, "You are the man!" (2 Samuel 11:27b-12:7a, NIV)

We have all had a David moment. We have all had a time or two or three or four… when we were completely unaware of something we did wrong. It takes a Nathan to set us straight. Each of us can be blinded to something in our lives, whether it be something we did wrong and are unaware, or something we are not doing that we are unaware we should be doing. There is a part of a great prayer in the 1979 Book of Common Prayer, "Have mercy upon us, most merciful Father; in your compassion forgive us our sins, known and unknown, things done and left undone;..."[26]

The 'thing' David did and is being called out for is his reprehensible behavior toward Uriah the Hittite. David is overcome by desire for Uriah's wife, Bathsheba. He sees her bathing one afternoon and must have her. He sends word about her and finds out she is Uriah's wife. Undeterred, he sends for her

---

[26] *The Book of Common Prayer*, 393.

and seduces her. A few weeks later Bathsheba sends word to David that she is pregnant. Uriah had been away at battle this whole time, fighting the Kings battles for him. David must fix the situation. So he calls for Uriah. He tries to entice Uriah to go sleep with his wife, but he will not. Uriah nobly cannot find pleasure while the rest of his men are struggling in battle. At his wits end, David makes a bad situation worse. He writes a note to Joab, the leader of his army, to force a fierce fighting battle with Uriah in the front, and in the midst of this battle have everyone withdraw from Uriah so he will be struck down and die. To top it all off, David delivers this note to Joab by the hand of...Uriah.

Who knows how David was justifying and rationalizing his actions in his head? The text does not say. Perhaps he thinks, "Well, I am the King. I have fought hard in the past. Surely God would not deny me the pleasure of a beautiful women." "I tried to fix this by having Uriah be with his wife." "No one can know the wrong I have committed. I am the King. I must always be strong and in the right." "I cannot fail in the eyes of others." "I am not the only one who would do this if they were in my situation." "Surely God forgives me."

Maybe David thought some of these things. If he did, then the only thing he was right on was the last thing. God does forgive him, but not because he is the favored King. No, it is because God deeply desires a greater relationship with all people. Once David is made aware of his sin (notice that the sin, or missing of the mark, began within him), then he is able to deeply feel the pain of his sin and have true remorse. He is able to enter into the forgiveness that God offers. In one of the saddest scenes in the Bible, the child to be born to David and Bathsheba dies. Yet grace abounds as their next child is Solomon, who goes on to be a great and wise King (with his own faults and shortcomings).

This story is about great sin, false justification, rationalization, and, eventually, repentance and forgiveness. It also teaches a powerful lesson about projection. A projection is, "The process by which one attributes one's own individual positive or negative characteristics, affects, and impulses to another person or group."[27] We project our shortcomings outside of ourselves, generally on someone else. David rationalized away his sin so well that he is unable to see it. When told the story about the rich man taking the one little precious ewe lamb of the poor man to be

---

[27] *APA Concise Dictionary of Psychology*, 400.

sacrificed for a guest, David explodes in anger. "Who could possibly do such a wretched thing?" David thinks. David declares the rich man deserves death. Nathan then lands into David pronouncing God's displeasure with David. "You are the man!" (2 Samuel 12:7) David then sees the sin in himself. Mirror meet face. Face meet mirror.

*Projections are tricky_*

If we know what projections are, then we often think we know when we are projecting. However, that is the hidden power of projection. The whole point of a projection is that you are unaware you are doing it. The moment you are aware of a projection and take it seriously, then it ceases to be a projection. You then have the choice of how to respond. It can also be true that one will continually project over and over again, even if made aware of the projection. We can continually project onto others the same things in similar situations, unable to learn important lessons and apply them. This often happens in relationship. We continually hit brick wall after brick wall with people and wonder why everybody has the same problem. When in reality it is something inside us we need to examine.

Generally, we are given clues by God of when we are projecting. If there is something about someone else that makes us so angry we can't stand it, then it is likely a shortcoming we have in common with the other person that we unknowingly dislike in ourselves. This does not mean that we are wrong in our assessment about the other person. We may or may not be right about that person's shortcomings. However, the fact that another person's shortcomings make us so angry is a clear indication that we need to do some serious self-analysis.

Jesus specifically teaches about projection

Jesus famously said, "You hypocrite, first take the plank out of your own eye, and then you will see clearly to remove the speck from your brother's eye." (Matthew 7:5) Jesus knows that we are capable of recognizing, understanding, and accepting our own faults. After this self-examination we are then able to see the sins and faults of others more clearly. As a result, they will not push

105

our buttons as much, and we can lovingly help that other person instead of judging or condemning them.

Projections result in many feelings

Projections can also elicit very positive feelings, sometimes over-the-top feelings. When we unknowingly sense that someone else has a trait we deeply admire and desperately want, then we project tremendous positive feelings on that person. We tend to overly idolize that person instead of simply admiring them. Every four years I am amazed at how many people put unrealistic hopes in political candidates. Some well-meaning people attach themselves to a specific candidate because that candidate appears to have something special (whether they do or not is up for debate). These people begin to see a savior to all their problems. Deep down it is something they see in the other person that they want to claim for themselves. Some people say, "that person has the 'it' factor." Their inability to connect with that part of themselves makes them unconsciously attracted to that person. They look externally for something they seek internally. These people often cry their eyes out when the person they projected such good feelings upon disappoints them. Notice I wrote "when" not "if." All people we project upon in this way will eventually fail us because we have unfairly elevated a common human being to God-like status. It is all because we are unable to own the qualities we desire in ourselves.

This is not only true of political figures that we put on pedestals. It can be true of anyone we unconsciously elevate. They can be religious leaders, business leaders, athletes, singers, or even people close to us. How many people do we have to unwisely build up to the sky, only to see them crash hard to the ground later? Can we not recognize when we are doing this, become conscious of what we truly desire, and then be able to care for another as a human being with strengths and weaknesses of their own?

Projections can be very painful in close intimate relationships. Let me give you a hint. If you are so over-the-top in love with someone else, then you are projecting something on that person. It does not mean that they are not wonderful; it just means you need to examine what this person can teach you about yourself. When these projections start to melt away, then true human relationship can begin to happen, by the grace of

God. Unfortunately, many people leave when the shine and luster of the initial false relationship begins to fade. They leave just when things are becoming truly human.

Learning to look in the mirror

In 1994 I had many projections, as I do now (I hope I am better at recognizing them and learning from them). I was a recent college graduate with a Bachelor of Science degree in psychology. So of course I knew all about projections, right? I thought I did. I also thought I was at the most mature state of all the stage models I was taught in Psychology classes. I thought to myself, "Of course since I know them I must be much more mature than others." Now, I did know some things, but I really didn't know them internally. Nancy became my Nathan. Everyone needs a Nathan in their life.

People I could not stand were people who were judgmental, condescending, self-righteous, and superficial. I remember one day coming to a session with Nancy complaining about a well-known politician. "I just can't stand that guy. He always lies and is superficial. Moreover, he almost brags about being this way. It is all about 'how to spin' and 'image is everything.' I just can't stand people who are fake." Nancy looked at me and lovingly said, "Boy, you really don't like it when you are unconsciously superficial, do you?" Bang! Right between the eyes. Mirror meet face. Face meet mirror.

"Exposed for all to see." Tuesday 10/25/94.

I dreamed I showed up to Drew's office and I was just in my boxer shorts and he was mad at me for doing this (showing up to his office like this.) I tried to avoid him, but then he saw me. So he said that was it, "I am going to get you fired." So we went down to the lobby and I got really angry and started a fight with him. He seemed bigger, but I would not back down. I wound up winning and when I did he apologized. I asked him why he did not like me, and he confessed it was that he liked the youth worker before me and when the youth worker before me left he did not say his proper goodbyes, and he didn't want the same thing happening twice. When he went to go to the elevator, I ran to tell him not to ever forget to repent or something. I was very happy I had won out.

Nancy - How did you feel in the dream?
Me - At first I felt embarrassed, then resolute, and at the end happy.
Nancy - Who is Drew?
Me - Drew is one of the parents of the youth at Church.
Nancy - Do you like him?
Me - He is not a bad guy, but he is not my cup of tea.
Nancy - Why is that?
Me - He is wealthy and he acts like a know it all.
Nancy - Hmm. Too self-righteous for your tastes, huh?
Me - Yeah, I guess.
Nancy - Have you been in conflict with him before?
Me - Yeah, he helps out with the youth group and sometimes tests my authority as the leader. One time I bet him.
Nancy - How so?
Me - We were taking the youth group on an outing. I said we would be to the place in twenty minutes. He said there is no way with the traffic. I bet him and won the bet.
Nancy - So why do you think you show up to his office in your underwear?
Me - I guess it means I feel insecure around him.
Nancy - Or insecure in the part of you he represents.
Me - Yeah, I guess.
Nancy - Do you like it when you are self-righteous?
Me - No. Of course not.
Nancy - Do you think you are self-righteous often?
Me - No. I hope not.
Nancy - But you can be self-righteous?
Me - Yeah.
Nancy - So why do you think you can become self-righteous?
Me - I don't know. I guess I don't like it when someone challenges me.
Nancy - What do you want to do when you are challenged?
Me - I want to beat them. Not beat them up, but just beat them at their own game or show that they are wrong.
Nancy - Does that sound like a good solution?
Me - It does at the time.
Nancy - Maybe the dream is challenging you to learn to respond differently?

Me - Yeah, maybe.
Nancy - So in the dream you get in a fight with him?
Me - Yeah.
Nancy - And you think he is bigger than you?
Me - Yeah, he is not bigger than me in real life, but he is bigger than me in the dream.
Nancy - Why do you think that is?
Me - Because he is a big obstacle for me?
Nancy -I think so. But you are able to talk through your problem with him.
Me - Yeah, he told me in the dream he was sad the former youth leader left without him saying goodbye.
Nancy - It feels better when you know why someone is acting a certain way?
Me - Yeah, I guess...I mean yeah, definitely.
Nancy - What did Jesus say, "Take the plank out of your own eye..."
Me - "then you will see clearly to remove the speck from your brother's eye." (Matthew 7:5)
Nancy - Easier said than done, huh?
Me - Yeah, definitely. Do I need to do anything?
Nancy - No. Not unless you feel the need to apologize to someone to reconcile. This is a dream for your own learning.
Me - It doesn't have anything to do with the real Drew.
Nancy - Not directly, although sometimes dreams guide you to certain things with others. Most of the time they are for your learning, and by learning internally it will positively affect all your external relationships.
Me - So I don't need to do anything?
Nancy - No. Just keep paying attention and learning. Keep the mirror in your face. Have you heard that phrase?
Me - Yeah, I think so.

"Halloween villain in the Cathedral." Wednesday, 11/9/94.

I was in the Cathedral and Michael Myers broke in and was going to do some damage. I caught him and then chased him down the steps. Afterwards I didn't want to stay in the Cathedral for fear that he would retaliate.

Nancy - How did you feel in the dream?
Me - Scared.

Nancy - That is what I thought. Who is this Michael Myers?

Me - He is the bad guy in the *Halloween* scary movie series.

Nancy - Is he the one with the hockey mask?

Me - No. That is Jason Vorhees. Michael Myers is the guy with the plain face mask. He is insane and killed his sister or something. Every Halloween he goes and looks for people to kill.

Nancy - What does Halloween mean to you?

Me - It's a time when people dress up to have fun.

Nancy - Maybe people secretly or unconsciously want to be someone else?

Me - Maybe. It is also the night before All Saints Day.

Nancy - So a night of sin before celebrating the saints of the church. Ha. Ha.

Me - An interesting contrast.

Nancy - Indeed. So, in the dream Michael breaks into a cathedral. What does a cathedral mean to you?

Me - It is a place of worship. It is also central to the Church because it is where the Bishop has his 'Cathedra' or seat.

Nancy - What does a Bishop mean to you?

Me - A Bishop is a defender of the faith.

Nancy - So this central place of worship is being broken into?

Me - I guess so.

Nancy - Doesn't the Bible say that our, "bodies are temples of the Holy Spirit." (1 Corinthians 6:19)

Me - Yes. I believe so.

Nancy - So something very destructive is breaking into your cathedral.

Me - Is that bad?

Nancy - We all have to get in touch with our dark side. The more unconscious of it we are, the more dangerous it can be. Women will often dream of a witch like figure. However, if we are in touch with our dark side it can help us and not be destructive. What do you feel is destructive in you?

Me - I have a pretty good temper?

Nancy - Do you try to squelch your anger or understand it?

Me - I squelch it.

Nancy - What about your faith? Do you ever feel it being attacked?

Me - That is why I am here, isn't it?

Nancy - In the dream you chase it away, but you are afraid it will come back. Is it better to face your destructive side and understand it? Or is it better to live in fear of it?

Me - I guess to try and understand it. But how do you understand something you are so afraid of?

Nancy - Well, it is there, inside us, whether we want to acknowledge it or not. The more we ignore it the more we project it out into the world and live in the extremes.

Me - Is that why some religious people try to be holier than thou?

Nancy - And always fail? Yes. We need to embrace the darkness within.

Me - Does that mean embrace evil?

Nancy - No, it is to be aware of our inner darkness so it can be brought into the light so we don't unconsciously project it out and it becomes evil, or we just see the bad in other people and not in ourselves.

Me - Do I need to do anything?

Nancy - You are doing something. Inner work is hard work. Becoming aware of our projections and darkness is hard work. Just keep paying attention. Your unconscious will guide you.

Reflection questions:
1. Have you ever been made aware of something you did wrong? How did you react?
2. What characteristics do you not like in other people? How are you like that?
3. What darkness in you are you afraid of? How can you bring that out into the light?

Chapter Thirteen: Burning Hearts

Now that same day two of them were going to a village called Emmaus, about seven miles from Jerusalem. They were talking with each other about everything that had happened. As they talked and discussed these things with each other, Jesus himself came up and walked along with them; but they were kept from recognizing him. He asked them, "What are you discussing together as you walk along?" They stood still, their faces downcast. One of them, named Cleopas, asked him, "Are you the only one visiting Jerusalem who does not know the things that have happened there in these days?" "What things?" he asked. "About Jesus of Nazareth," they replied. "He was a prophet, powerful in word and deed before God and all the people. The chief priests and our rulers handed him over to be sentenced to death, and they crucified him; but we had hoped that he was the one who was going to redeem Israel. And what is more, it is the third day since all this took place. In addition, some of our women amazed us. They went to the tomb early this morning but didn't find his body. They came and told us that they had seen a vision of angels, who said he was alive. Then some of our companions went to the tomb and found it just as the women had said, but they did not see Jesus." He said to them, "How foolish you are, and how slow to believe all that the prophets have spoken! Did not the Messiah have to suffer these things and then enter his glory?" And beginning with Moses and all the Prophets, he explained to them what was said in all the Scriptures concerning himself. As they approached the village to which they were going, Jesus continued on as if he were going farther. But they urged him strongly, "Stay with us, for it is nearly evening; the day is almost over." So he went in to stay with them.

When he was at the table with them, he took bread, gave thanks, broke it and began to give it to them. Then their eyes were opened and they recognized him, and he disappeared from their sight. They asked each other, "Were not our hearts burning within us while he talked with us on the road and opened the Scriptures to us?" (Luke 24:13-32, NIV)

"Were not our hearts burning within us..." Do we pay attention to the living Christ who is always with us? The road to Emmaus passage in Luke is one of the most powerful in the entire Bible. It teaches us a deep profound lesson about God being with us.

We often miss the grace of God all around us. We have been conditioned in our lives to focus on certain things. We focus on self, other people, world events, or material gain. We want life to be a certain way and if it is not then something is wrong or God is not with us. On the other hand, we all know that life is not perfect. We thus tend to settle. The eternal pessimist declares, "The only thing certain in life is death and taxes." Sometimes we go back and forth between wanting life to be a certain way, and settling for less because we think that is all there is. However, what if there was a third option? What if God was truly ever-present with us, begging for us to focus on God?

God surrounds us with love in unexpected ways

There is an old joke that goes something like this. There was a flood coming and a man was determined that God himself would be faithful and save him from drowning. As the rains began a police officer came by the house. He warned the man to leave. "A flood is coming," the officer said. The man replied, "I know. God will save me." As the waters rose the man had to go on his roof. A boat came by. The men in the boat yelled to the man, "Come, save yourself and jump into the boat!" "No, no, God will save me," protested the man. The waters continued to rise. Soon the man was forced to stand on top of the chimney. A helicopter went by. The pilot screamed, "Grab hold of the ladder and climb up to the helicopter. This is your last chance." The man stomped his foot, "No, no God will save me." The helicopter left and soon after the man drowned. When the man got to heaven he was very upset. He said to God, "God, I was so faithful to you! Why were you not faithful to me? Why did you let me drown?" God said,

"What are you talking about? I sent a police officer, a boat, and a helicopter to save you and you didn't take the help."

The story tells a truth. God often comes to us in ways we don't expect or in ways we think are not of God. Now I know what you are thinking. You are thinking that sometimes those are just random occurrences, and God does not always save. However, I have come to believe that God is always with us. Mick Jagger of The Rolling Stones often sings out, "You can't always get what you want, but if you try sometimes you just might find, you get what you need."[28] A spiritual way of saying this is, "God does not always answer things the way we want it, but God does give us what we need." I often say that, "If the goal in life is to be rich, twenty-five years old, beautiful, and healthy, then we all fail. None of us stays young, pretty, rich and healthy forever." However, if life is about an ever-deepening relationship with God, then all things that happen in life can be avenues to a deeper relationship with God. It is always process and journey. God is more concerned about surrounding us with sacrificial love, than about making things the way we think they ought to be.

This is what the road to Emmaus story is teaching us. The Risen living Christ is with us. However, we often don't see God. In the story two of Jesus' followers are walking away from Jerusalem. They probably want to get away from what has happened. As they walk along Jesus starts walking with them. For some reason they are kept from recognizing him. Who knows why this is the case? The text does not say why their eyes were kept from recognizing him. As they walk, Jesus asks them about what they are discussing. They ask Jesus, "Are you the only one visiting Jerusalem who does not know the things that have happened there in these days?" (Luke 24:18) Notice Jesus is the only one who truly knows all that has happened, but the two who are blinded think they know more than God does. Then they say something amazing, "But we had hoped that he was the one who was going to redeem Israel." (Luke 24:21) Now redemption has already taken place, and is taking place, yet once again they cannot see what God is really doing. Next, Jesus calls them foolish and explains all the scriptures in light of who he is. Christ has always been and will always be. As they come to Emmaus Jesus continues to keep going, but they urge him to stay. There is

---

[28] Rolling Stones, "You Can't Always Get What You Want," track 9 on *Let it Bleed*, Decca / London Records, 1969.

something about the love of God that when we begin to have it explained to us and we experience it, then we just want to continue to be around it. Jesus stays with them. Then in the breaking of the bread he is made known to them. The breaking of the bread is truly powerful. It is beyond explanation. Jesus then vanishes. The full truth of God can never be captured and contained. Finally, in retrospect, they claim, "Were not our hearts burning within us while he talked with us on the road and opened the Scriptures to us?" (Luke 24:32) We too often see God more clearly at work in the past, than we can see God at work in the present.

There is so much deep truth in the road to Emmaus story. Is this not the way Jesus still walks with us and teaches us in our lives if we pay attention? To me there are two lessons. First, we miss God when we sulk, and second we recognize God when we ask God to stay and be with us in the breaking of the bread.

Tear, tear...sniff, sniff

The two complain, "But we had hoped that he was the one who was going to redeem Israel." (Luke 24:21) Jesus responds, "How foolish you are, and how slow to believe..." (Luke 24:25) If it is not too blasphemous to put words in Jesus' mouth, I believe Jesus is basically saying, "Whayy!" In other words, quit whining and sulking and pay attention to the love you do see. We can all sulk. It is easy to do. The tricky thing is knowing when we are sulking and whining. I am the youngest of three brothers. It was my job to whine, and I didn't even know it. My brothers would say, "Quit whining." "I am not whining!" I would protest in the whiniest voice ever.

It is so easy to sulk and whine. Why doesn't God fix this, why doesn't God fix that? Why doesn't God cure world poverty? Why doesn't God make things perfect? When we focus in this way, like the two on the road to Emmaus, we will miss the sacrificial love all around us. Once again, God is more interested in surrounding us with love, than making things perfect the way we want them to be. Further, last I checked, God has given us plenty of resources to help many of our issues. Many of our issues are human-made. However, even in the tough times when God does not heal cancer, or God does not divert the tornado, or God does not help someone out of poverty, I still believe God is there. God is right

116

there surrounding us with love. It may be very difficult to see, but open the eyes of your heart as best you can and it is there.

Further, we are called to be people of faith and to take action with that faith. I love the adapted quote from George Bernard Shaw that Robert Kennedy made famous, "Some men see things as they are and say, why, I dream things that never were and say, why not." God desires we prayerfully listen, dream, and boldly act. When we do this we catch glimpses of the face that is walking right next to us.

"Take, eat."

Finally, we see God in the breaking of the bread. In Holy Communion we take the bread, bless it, break it, and share it. Jesus was taken, blessed, broken open on the cross, and thus shared. We as the body of Christ can be taken by God, blessed by God, broken, and I believe it is when we are broken that God can use us to share the love of God with each other. Henri Nouwen wrote an amazing reflection on this truth in his book *With Burning Hearts: A Meditation on the Eucharistic Life.*

There is nothing magical about Holy Communion. It is loving presence, not magic. Jesus is truly present, and when we pay attention it is deeply powerful. God feeds us. In Holy Communion we pray to God. We take simple gifts of bread and wine. We are reminded of the loving acts of Christ. Finally, we do it in community. That is powerful, and God is present. It truly feeds our souls. I am always amazed on Sunday afternoons. I almost always feel good. There is just something about receiving Holy Communion. It is the mystery of faith. It is the joy of Christ's presence.

We can also experience the power of God in the breaking of the bread in other ways. The breaking of the bread experience of God can happen even when we don't physically break bread. It can happen around a campfire singing a song. It can happen with a small group and some old Bibles. It can happen while reading a book with someone who feels alone. The breaking of the bread is anytime we take simple gifts, prayerfully offer ourselves to God, take note of the sacrificial love of Christ, and do it in community. It is the power of the living, loving, ever-present God.

Walking out from the desert

After a year or so with Nancy in dream analysis, my desert experience began to fade. I had hoped that I would have some knock-down, slain-in-the-Spirit moment, but that did not happen for me. There was no Saint Paul road-to-Damascus experience for me. I do believe that others have that kind of experience, but not all do, and I did not. I wanted a big "Aha" moment. Instead, I received little moments of grace on a long journey of gradual healing. For me the anxiety and awful thoughts faded as I became more and more aware of God within. I was a new person, that was for sure. I continued to do inner dream analysis for several years to continue my formation, always being guided by the Holy Spirit.

As I look back now, my experience was much like the two on the road to Emmaus. I was walking along sulking and in sheer agony. My eyes were kept for some reason from seeing Jesus all around, but he was definitely there. Christ was surrounding me with sacrificial love when I visited Reverend Ben, started a prayer group with friends, went out west, sought the love of friends and family, and, finally, when I started listening to God transforming my life from within through dream analysis. If I had not had this experience I do not know where I would be. Perhaps I would be a different person, but this was the path God had for me.

I do not believe that God causes tragedy just to teach us. Truth be told, I don't even try to figure out why some things happen anymore. It is what it is. It is always process, always journey. We can't change the cards we are dealt or even know who the dealer is sometimes. Life is too complex for us to completely figure out, and I do not believe God wants us to find the answer to all life's questions. We are, however, called to be present and faithful. I do believe that God does walk with us, teaching us through the difficult times in life. Sometimes there is dryness, sometimes there is joy, and God is in the midst of all of it.

My new God voice

The way I experienced God within myself never returned to the way it had been. I lost my childhood faith for good. Not that having a childhood faith is wrong. We are whore wo arc, and that is ok. However, things are not as simple as consulting an inner feeling every time I need support. My inner life is much richer, deeper, and constantly moving forward. I developed a more discerning way of listening to God. I still trust my gut and listen for the love of God in my heart, but I have learned to do this more intentionally. Further, I have learned to listen for God in many different ways, much like a relationship with another person. It has grown to be understood in new ways. I have learned to look at my relationship with God through prayer, faithful reading of scripture, worship in community, reaching out to others, and, of course, paying attention to dreams.

First, I am more intentional with prayer. If you want to know someone better, then the most important thing to do is to be in frequent conversation and LISTENING TO that person. It is the same with God. Now I am not always faithful, but I pray much more consistently. These prayer times are not always full of deep insight, but sometimes they are. Further, I do believe that the more I pray the more I notice God all around. The more I make my life known to God (which is more me knowing that I am making God aware), the more at peace I feel that God is in my life. Prayer is conversation with God.

Second, I am faithful in reading scripture. If you had a friend who had multiple books written about them, wouldn't you want to read them? You could learn a lot about that friend from the experiences others had with them. The same is true for God. When we read the scriptures we are reading others' experience with the living, loving God. This also helps us see God in our lives more clearly. I understand the Bible as a window to the living God.

Third, I worship in community. If you had a friend wouldn't you want to be with others who know that person? Further, wouldn't you want to speak well and praise that person with those who love that person? This is what we do in worship. We praise and glorify God with others who know God. God deeply desires to be praised.

Fourth, I help others in need as best I can. Not that I didn't do this before, but I truly now see it as a way of deepening my relationship with God. If you had a friend, wouldn't you want to help the loved ones of that friend as best you can? In this way we learn about the love of the friend. Same is also true of God. When we help people who God loves (which is all of us), then we come to know God's love better. God wants us to help each other. God is a God of sacrificial love and relationship, always.

Finally, I pay attention to dreams. This of course is what this book is all about. I believe that John Sanford and many others were right when they called dreams, 'God's forgotten language.'[29]

A final prayer

"When he was at the table with them, he took bread, gave thanks, broke it and began to give it to them. Then their eyes were opened and they recognized him, and he disappeared from their sight." (Luke 24:30, 31) May we all know that we are blessed by Christ's presence often and always. We are never able to contain it. Do not our hearts burn within for the love of God? I pray that they might. Amen.

Reflection questions:
1. What difficult times have you lived through? Can you look back now and see where God was with you?
2. Where do you think God is walking with you now? When is it easy or hard to see?
3. How has your understanding of God deepened throughout your life?

---

[29] Sanford, *Dreams: God's Forgotten Language*, 41.

Bibliography

APA Concise Dictionary of Psychology. Washington DC: American Psychological Association, 2009. print.

The Book of Common Prayer. New York: The Church Hymnal Corporation, 1979. print.

Bly, Robert. *Iron John: A Book about Men.* New York: Vintage Books, 1990. print.

Bowden, John and Richardson, Alan, ed. *The Westminster Dictionary of Christian Theology.* Philadelphia: Westminster Press, 1983. print.

Brown, Raymond E. *An Introduction to the New Testament.* New York: Doubleday, 1997. print.

Buechner, Frederick. *The Magnificent Defeat.* San Francisco: HarperCollins, 1966. print.

Buechner, Frederick. *Wishful Thinking: A Theological ABC.* San Francisco: HarperCollins, 1973. print.

Cameron, Julia. *The Artist's way: A Spiritual Path to Higher Creativity.* New York: G.P. Putnam's Sons, 1992. print.

Carmen, Ronnie Del and Docter, Pete. *Inside Out.* DVD. Directed by Pete Docter. Burbank, CA: Walt Disney / Pixar Pictures, 2015. film.

Childress, James F., and Macquarrie, John, ed. *The Westminster Dictionary of Christian Ethics.* Philadelphia: The Westminster Press, 1986. print.

Coleman, Andrew M. *Dictionary of Psychology*. Oxford: Oxford University Press, 2001. print.

Cornwall, Judson and Smith, Stelman, ed. *The Exhaustive Dictionary of Bible Names.* Alachua, FL: Bridge-Logos, 1998. print.

Dosick, Rabbi Wayne. *Living Judaism: The complete guide to Jewish Belief, Tradition, and Practice.* San Francisco: HarperCollins, 1995. print.

Flew, Antony G.N. & Habermas, Gary R. *Did Jesus Rise from the Dead: The Resurrection Debate.* San Francisco: Harper & Row, 1987. print.

Goyer, David S. and Nolan, Christopher. *Man of Steel.* DVD. Directed by Zack Snyder. Burbank, CA: Warner Bros. Pictures, 2013. film.

Green, Jay P. and Robinson, Maurice, ed. *A Concise Lexicon to the Biblical Languages.* Lafayette, IN: Sovereign Grace Publishers, 1987. print.

Hays, Richard B. *The Moral Vision of the New Testament.* San Francisco: HarperCollins, 1996. print.

Hollis, James. *The Middle Passage: From Misery to Meaning in Midlife.* Toronto: Inner City Books, 1993. print.

Jung, C. G., and Anthony Storr, ed. *The Essential Jung: Selected Writings.* Princeton, NJ: Princeton University Press, 1999. print.

Led Zeppelin, "Good Times / Bad Times," track 1 on Led Zeppelin, Atlantic, 1968. record.

Lewis, C.S. *Mere Christianity.* New York: Macmillan, 1962. print.

Little, Paul E. *Know Why You Believe.* Downers Grove, IL: InterVarsity Press, 1988. print.

McDowell, Josh. *More Than A Carpenter.* Wheaton, IL: Living Books, 1977. print.

Mitchell, Leonel L. *Praying Shapes Believing.* Hamburg, PA.: Morehouse Publishing, 1985. print.

Morris, Henry M. *Science and The Bible.* Chicago: Moody Press, 1979. print.

Nouwen, Henri J.M. *The Wounded Healer.* Garden City, New York: Doubleday, 1972. print.

Nouwen, Henri J.M. *With Burning Hearts: A Meditation on The Eucharistic Life.* Maryknoll, New York: Orbis Books, 1994. print.

O'Day, Gail R. "The Gospel of John." in *The New Interpreter's Bible: Volume IX,* senior editor Leander E. Keck, 493-865. Nashville: Abingdon Press, 1995. print.

Perkins, Pheme. "The Gospel of Mark." in *The New Interpreter's Bible: Volume VIII,* senior editor Leander E. Keck, 509-733. Nashville: Abingdon Press, 1995. print.

Rayner, John A. *The First Century of Piqua, Ohio.* Piqua, Ohio: Magee Brothers Co., 1916. print.

Rolling Stones, "You Can't Always Get What You Want," track 9 on *Let it Bleed*, Decca / London Records, 1969. record.

Sanford, John A. *Dreams: God's Forgotten Language.* New York: Crossroad, 1968. print.

Sanford, John A. *Healing Body and Soul.* Louisville, KY: Westminster/John Knox Press, 1992. print.

Sanford, John A. *The Kingdom Within.* San Francisco: HarperCollins, 1991. print.

Shaw, George Bernard. *Back to Methuselah, act I, Selected Plays of Bernard Shaw.* New York: Dodd Mead, 1949. print.

Silverstein, Shel. *The Giving Tree.* San Francisco: Harper & Row, 1964. print.

Willimon, William H. *Sighing for Eden: sin, Evil & The Christian Faith.* Nashville: Abingdon Press, 1985. print.

ZZ Top, "Sharp Dressed Man," track 3 on *Eliminator*, Warner Bros., 1983. Record

Printed in Great Britain
by Amazon